Ensouled Region, Shining

Ensouled Region, Shining

The Poems of Fray Luis de León

Fray Luis de León

Translated by
H. L. HIX

RESOURCE *Publications* · Eugene, Oregon

ENSOULED REGION, SHINING
The Poems of Fray Luis de León

Resource Publications
An Imprint of Wipf and Stock Publishers
199 W. 8th Ave., Suite 3
Eugene, OR 97401

www.wipfandstock.com

PAPERBACK ISBN: 979-8-3852-7312-6
HARDCOVER ISBN: 979-8-3852-7313-3
EBOOK ISBN: 979-8-3852-7314-0

Contents

Acknowledgments

I AM GRATEFUL TO the late Kevin Larsen for introducing me to the poetry of Fray Luis, and for encouraging me in this work. *Bien eres generoso / pimpollo de ilustríssimos mayores.*

The various elements of this manuscript were brought together and revised in the shelter of the Birch Creek Residency Program. I am grateful to the Program, especially in the person of its Director, Adam Bateman, for *la casa / en el campo deleytoso / con sólo Dios se compassa.*

I *would* be grateful to Spitball and Tenpin, but for *los abrojos agudos en tus almas.*

A few of these translations have enjoyed previous publication, for which I am grateful to the editors of the following journals: *Measure* ("Life Apart"), *Catch Up* ("On the Ascension"), *Borderlands* ("Quiet Night"), *Rowboat* ("Another Mode"; "On Release from Prison"), and *Taos Journal of International Poetry and Art* ("In the Highest Sphere").

And Kate. *¡Durasse en tu reposo / sin ser restituido / jamás aqueste baxo y vil sentido!*

Introduction

1. WHY THE POETRY OF FRAY LUIS DE LEÓN MATTERS TODAY

When canonical literary works enjoy esteem as "Great Books," their advocates typically recommend them on the basis of their having "stood the test of time," by which the advocates mean that the works have *survived* from their origin to the present day, enjoyed relatively wide and fairly consistent readership in the past, occasioned critical discussion, and received commendation from purported experts. If that rationale were sound, if time indeed conferred worth, then the old would rightly be presumed worthy, and the new would need yet to prove itself worthy. But grant, instead, Jared Carter's blunt declaration at the end of one of his poems, that "The purpose of poetry is to tell us about life"[1]: that premise would shift the burden of proof of validity and relevance from new poetry onto old. For an old poem to tell me about life as it *is*, not only about life as it *once was*, life as it is would have to be *like*, not only *continuous with*, life as it was, and at least prima facie this appears not to be the case.

Fray Luis de León (1527–1591) wrote his poems in another country, more than four centuries ago. The list of differences between life as it was for him and life as it is for us now is indefinitely long. He died before Charles Babbage originated the programmable computer, before James Watt had patented a steam engine,

1. Carter, *After the Rain*, 24.

before Isaac Newton had formulated his three laws of motion, before Shakespeare had written *Hamlet*, before Jamestown was settled. His birth was closer to Columbus' sailing the ocean blue than the present day is to Neil Armstrong's one giant step for mankind. So differently furnished was his world (no smart phones, no TVs, no airplanes, no bicycles, no supermarkets, no flush toilets) and so differently understood (no Einstein yet, no Darwin, no Adam Smith, no "liberté, égalité, fraternité"), that it is not obvious what his experience has in common with ours. Consequently, it is not obvious what *his* poetry might tell us about *our* lives, and thus what reason there might be for translating his poetry, or for reading it. What makes it "news that stays news"? His poetry was written in a distant *then*; what makes what his poetry tells us about life true *of*, and true *to*, life now? A translator inviting you to devote time and attention here and now to work this old and distant owes you an account of what might make it worth your while to do so.

This poetry *does* pass the "Great Books" test. Fray Luis is recognized as a major figure in Spanish literature, and his poetry enjoys canonical status, so translators and others have offered as rationales for interest in his work numerous variations on the theme of its having stood the test of time. For instance, in *The Penguin Book of Spanish Verse*, J. M. Cohen introduces Fray Luis by noting that his poems "are modelled on Horace, and are concerned with the contrast between earthly life and the spiritual reality." But in expressing that concern, they are not, Cohen suggests, typical of the poetry of his day. They do not simply reflect cultural expectations. "They are far more monumental and far less ornate than the poetry fashionable in his day."[2] Similarly, Eugenio Florit points out that, though Fray Luis's "poetic output was small," many of his poems "are without equal in Spanish poetry." They "reflect the contemplative spirit of their author and the intensity of his love of God"; they are admired, Florit notes, for their "serenity and sincerity" and "for the sobriety and clarity of their style, as well as for the sublimity of their ideas."[3]

2. Cohen, *Spanish Verse*, xii.

3. Florit, *Spanish Poetry*, 45.

Not all such rationales are unqualified. Billy Collins, for example, in his introduction to Edith Grossman's anthology of "Golden Age" poetry, implies that the poems are derivative: Collins calls Fray Luis a "kind of Christian Horace," who "praised the simple life of the countryside" only because Horace had done so, even though Fray Luis himself "hardly experienced plain-living in his time."[4] Grossman for her part gives only a muted appreciation, confining Fray Luis to a role in an historical movement: he is, she says, "generally considered a leading poet in the far-reaching 'Christianization' of the Renaissance in Spain during the sixteenth century."[5] Still, even such qualified rationales rest on canonicity; *that*'s what they are qualifying. "It's not perfect," their remarks imply of the poetry, "but it has held up."

My distrust of a "Great Books" approach to literature precludes my appealing to "greatness" or other terms related to canonicity, and precludes my taking durability for relevance. (I identify with *Middlemarch*'s Dorothea more than I trust to its Casaubon.) The reason to read Fray Luis's poetry (the answer to the question why one might be interested in a 400-year-old artifact) is not, I contend, that it has hung around, or that other readers have thought well of it, but that it tells me about life. *My* life, *now*. There may be many ways in which it tells me about life (and if it sustains multiple readings, surely there *must* be). Here, though, I focus on one in particular, sufficient by itself to establish these poems' relevance, and a clue to which lies in the combination of two biographical facts about Fray Luis.

First, he devoted his adult life to the Church. Sent at age fourteen to study canon law at Salamanca, he soon left to enter the Order of the Hermits of St Augustine, into which order "he made his solemn profession on 29 January 1544."[6] He took a master's degree in theology in 1560. He remained in the Order, fulfilling his vocation, for the rest of his life. But the second biographical fact stands in dramatic tension with the first. On 27 March 1572,

4. Collins, "Introduction," xix.

5. Grossman, *The Golden Age*, 102.

6. Thompson, *The Strife of Tongues*, 5.

Fray Luis was arrested by an officer of the Spanish Inquisition. He was found guilty, and spent four years in prison as a result. He was imprisoned, that is, by the very Church to the service of which he had devoted — was devoting — his life.

The combination of spiritual vocation and imprisonment by the Inquisition stands as existential evidence of what I want to call "box four thinking," and insofar as his poems, like his life, manifest box four thinking they offer challenge and edification to readers of *any* time period, including our own, and in any cultural context, ours no less than his. What is at stake, in other words, is not context-dependent: like the law of gravity, box four does not vary in its applicability or force according to developments in human technologies or changes in human social arrangements. An explanation of my assertion can begin with the following table, intended to identify a point of commonality between Fray Luis's time and our own time, and thus provide a basis for asserting the ongoing (and especially the *contemporary*) relevance of his work.

		Immanence Is Ultimate	Transcendence Is Ultimate
Authority Is Final	1. Advocate	1.1: Hobbes	2.1: Aquinas
	2. Exemplar	1.2: Stalin	2.2: "the war on terror"
	3. Epistemological ideal	1.3: clarity	2.3: certainty
	4. Aesthetic ideal	1.4: order	2.4: simplicity
	5. Ideal posture	1.5: loyalty	2.5: piety
	6. Private danger	1.6: hypocrisy	2.6: dogmatism
	7. Manifestation	1.7: dictatorship	2.7: holy war
	8. Public danger	1.8: tyranny/ enslavement	2.8: jingoism
	9. Impediment	1.9: How *sustain* authority?	2.9: How *select* authority?
	10. Limit question	1.10: What *confers* authority?	2.10: What about alternatives?

Authority Is Provisional	1. Advocate	3.1: Machiavelli	4.1: Augustine
	2. Exemplar	3.2: market economy	4.2: Socrates
	3. Epistemological ideal	3.3: profit	4.3: mystery
	4. Aesthetic ideal	3.4: brand identity	4.4: sublimity
	5. Ideal posture	3.5: self-interest	4.5: reverence
	6. Private danger	3.6: relativism	4.6: insecurity
	7. Manifestation	3.7: wealth	4.7: civil disobedience
	8. Public danger	3.8: monopoly	4.8: anarchy
	9. Impediment	3.9: How secure one's gains?	4.9: How rest?decide?commit?
	10. Limit question	3.10: Is there no intrinsic value?	4.10: What assurance is there?

I present this chart only as a means of articulating why Fray Luis has ongoing pertinence, not as an end in itself. It could be thought-provoking, I believe, to explore it thoroughly on its own terms, but here I sketch only the minimal outline necessary to arrive at the point I wish to make about Fray Luis. The chart is "strong" in the sense that it divisions are exhaustive and mutually exclusive. Both horizontal and vertical divisions are either/ors: either immanence is ultimate or transcendence is, either authority is final or it is provisional. Consequently, *everyone* is, in principle, in one and only one of the four boxes. The chart is "weak" in that (a) humans are inconsistent (so I might *say* transcendence is ultimate, for instance, but *act* as if immanence were, or I might treat authority as final when it is convenient to do so, and as provisional when it is not), and (b) there is wide range for variation in how one defines/understands the terms (so I might understand the terms in such a way that I would place myself in box two, say, and you might understand the terms in such a way that you would place me in box one). That most of us, in practice, "cheat" by wiggling from box to box does not prevent distinguishing the boxes from proposing an ideal: the more clearly I "see" the differences, the better prepared I am to *choose* a box rather than be pushed into one, and to achieve moral/intellectual consistency by remaining in the chosen box rather than moving according to convenience, or just unreflectively, from box to box.

Here in briefest summary is what I mean by each quadrant in the chart.

1. If I regard immanence as ultimate — if nothing "above" the world supervenes upon the world — but I regard authority as final, then my viewpoint resembles that articulated at length by Thomas Hobbes in *Leviathan*. Hobbes depicts as disastrous the result of lack of final authority (and thus denies boxes 3 and 4) in his book's most famous passage. There he claims that "it is manifest, that during the time men live without a common Power to keep them all in awe, they are in that condition which is called Warre,"[7] in which "every man is Enemy to every man,"[8] and therefore there is no place for industry, culture, arts, and other human goods, but there is instead "continuall feare, and danger of violent death," and human life is "solitary, poore, nasty, brutish, and short." To prevent this worst of all conditions for humans, we must, Hobbes argues, defer to a Sovereign, but (here he rules out box 2) that deference entails a denial of transcendence. Even if "God Almighty can speak to a man," yet "he obliges no man to beleeve he hath done so to him that pretends it."[9] Since "Miracles now cease, we have no sign left,"[10] and since "Soveraigns in their own Dominions are the sole Legislators,"[11] the "transcendent" reduces to nothing other than what human authority — the sovereign — says it is. The

7. Hobbes, *Leviathan*, 185.
8. Hobbes, *Leviathan*, 186.
9. Hobbes, *Leviathan*, 411.
10. Hobbes, *Leviathan*, 414.
11. Hobbes, *Leviathan*, 415.

transcendent is not transcendent at all, only one guise of human authority.

2. One case for box two is given by Thomas Aquinas. Aquinas regards transcendence as ultimate (thus ruling out boxes 1 and 3): there is a God, by Whom the world is governed, and God is transcendent. In Aquinas' own words, "the universal end of all things is the Universal Good; Which is good of Itself by virtue of Its Essence, Which is the very essence of goodness; whereas a particular good is good by participation. Now it is manifest that in the whole created universe there is not a good which is not such by participation. Wherefore that good which is the end of the whole universe must be a good outside the universe."[12] The things of creation reflect in their nature this Universal Good. Humans, who have reason and free will, must exercise those capacities in order to participate in the Universal Good. Aquinas rules out box 4 by contending that human capacities and institutions are adequate to this Good. Natural Law endows humans with the capacity to enact Eternal Law, the principle of Universal Good, and the Church and Scripture communicate Eternal Law in terms appropriate to human capacities. In Aquinas' own formulation, "God has the design of the government of all things," but "this government will be so much the better in the degree the things governed are brought to perfection. Now it is a greater perfection for a thing to be good in itself and also the cause of goodness in others, than only to be good in itself. Therefore God so governs things that He makes some of them to be causes of others in government; as a master, who not only imparts knowledge to his pupils, but gives also the faculty of teaching others."[13] Human government, by realizing divine government, has final authority. (Recall that Aquinas does not assume that government means *secular* government.)

12. Aquinas, *Summa Theologica*, Ia q. 103 a. 2.

13. Aquinas, *Summa Theologica*, Ia q. 103 a. 6.

3. Box three receives one clear characterization in Machiavelli. For him, "the chief foundations of all states" are not the fruits of divine dispensation, but "good laws and good arms."[14] How we live and how we ought to live are radically different, and how we ought to live is altogether ineffectual: "he who abandons what is done for what ought to be done, will rather learn to bring about his own ruin than his preservation."[15] No God, no Justice oversees human affairs. Boxes 2 and 4 are ruled out: there is no transcendence, no Authority over authority. For Machiavelli, it is only a logical consequence that box 1 is also ruled out. In the absence of enforcement by the transcendent, nothing makes any authority final: authority is provisional, always *made up*. His response to the ultimacy of the immanent is the opposite of Hobbes's: for Hobbes, the absence of transcendent enforcement of authority means I should defer to authority for self-preservation; for Machiavelli, the absence of transcendent enforcement means I should seize authority for myself, for self-benefit.

4. Box four finds one articulation in the work of St. Augustine. There are other articulations, such as Kierkegaard's distinction between Christendom — box three, in which "we have become 'knowing' about Christ,"[16] in which we have transcendence on secure (final) authority — and Christianity — box four, in which we are "aware, facing the offense of the contradiction"[17] that inheres in affirming transcendence without any final authority on which to base the affirmation. I choose Augustine here, though, because Fray Luis was an Augustinian monk. For Augustine, boxes 1 and 3 are summarily ruled out: transcendence, not immanence, is ultimate. God — Augustine's personification of the transcendent — "is the light, the melody, the fragrance, the brilliance that space

14. Machiavelli, *Prince*, 72.

15. Machiavelli, *Prince*, 84.

16. Kierkegaard, *Practice in Christianity*, 35.

17. Kierkegaard, *Practice in Christianity*, 136.

> cannot contain, a sound that time cannot carry away, a perfume that no breeze disperses, a taste undiminished by eating, a clinging together that no satiety will sunder."[18] Yet, unlike Aquinas' confidence that human authority (for Aquinas, the Church) reveals and fulfills the transcendent robustly, for Augustine matters are more complicated, in a way that rules out box 2, and leaves only box 4 available. The transcendent cannot be reduced to the immanent. When Augustine asks "what is this God?," he receives consistent replies from the earth, the sea, and the animals: "We are not your God. Look above us." There is transcendence, and it alone has (and *is*) authority. No human authority can adequately represent it.

Fray Luis, then, on grounds that resemble those articulated by Augustine, is willing to enter into vocation — service of God, the transcendent, the ultimate — but *un*willing to accept as final an authority — the Inquisition — that claimed adequately to represent the transcendent.

The quadrants of the chart are not arbitrary quiz-show categories; they designate forms of understanding life experience and criteria for decision-making. The choice of quadrant is not an idle one, not free-floating opinion or a wholly subjective matter of taste. Choosing box 1, 2 , or 3 is a mistake *with consequences.* It was so during Fray Luis's lifetime, it is now, and it will be ever.

Amartya Sen's *Identity and Violence* offers a clear and forceful example of how a conceptual error can result in harm to oneself and to others. Sen points out that, although group affiliations participate in the construction of individual identities, no human's identity is composed exclusively of affiliation with one group. (Sen's "small sample of diverse categories to each of which I may simultaneously belong" is vivid: "I can be, at the same time, an Asian, and Indian citizen, a Bengali with Bangladeshi ancestry, an American or British resident, an economist, a dabbler in philosophy, an author, a Sanskritist, a strong believer in secularism and democracy, a man, a feminist, a heterosexual, a defender of

18. Augustine, *Confessions*, 215.

gay and lesbian rights, with a nonreligious lifestyle, from a Hindu background, a non-Brahmin, and a nonbeliever in an afterlife."[19]) Central to my decisions and to my effects on others is the arranging and prioritizing of these various affiliations, in ways appropriate to my ideals and to the context. Sen's point is that if I regard myself and/or others as identified exclusively by one affiliation, I severely restrict the possibilities for dialogue, and I further the conditions for violence. If, for example, I reduce your identity exclusively to your being Muslim (one group affiliation to which, in post-9/11 U.S. public discourse, identities are often reduced), and my own identity exclusively to being a Christian, then I have eliminated summarily all the common ground — perhaps we both are U.S. citizens, or live in the same neighborhood, or have children in the same school, and in any case we both are human beings — on the basis of which we might identify common cause. I have cast you exclusively as one of "them" rather than as one of "us." *A conceptual error* (reducing identity to only *one* of the numerous variables that together compose identity) *results in harm to myself and to others* (diminishing the basis for dialogue and enhancing conditions for violence). Marilynne Robinson makes the same point when she explicates "a fundamental shift in American consciousness. The Citizen has become the Taxpayer. In consequence of this shift, public assets are now public burdens."[20] The shift is a harmful conceptual error because Citizen and Taxpayer behave differently, in fulfillment of opposed ideals: "While the Citizen can entertain aspirations for the society as a whole and take pride in its achievements, the Taxpayer, as presently imagined, simply does not want to pay taxes."[21]

I contend that something analogous holds in regard to the distinction I am making here by means of the chart. The chart identifies three conceptual errors: denying the ultimacy of transcendence, and treating as final a human authority (box 1); recognizing the ultimacy of transcendence, but still treating non-transcendent

19. Sen, *Identity and Violence*, 19.

20. Robinson, *What Are We*, 84–85.

21. Robinson, *What Are We*, 85.

authority as final (box 2); denying the ultimacy of transcendence, and regarding all human authority as provisional (box 3). Each results in concomitant harm: tyranny in the first case, jingoism in the second, monopoly in the third.

The ill consequence of box 1, of course, is well captured by the familiar adage, "power corrupts; absolute power corrupts absolutely." Authority unchecked may be, as Hobbes argues, a way to deflect civil war, but that does not prevent its being also the formula for tyranny.

The ill consequence of box 2 is that if I believe both that transcendence is ultimate and that authority is final (that it communicates or is adequate to transcendence), I will be inclined to do as the United States did in the aftermath of September 11: appeal to the transcendent on behalf of my own (immanent) cause and against yours. Since there are many authorities claiming to communicate the transcendent, I will choose my preferred authority over yours, and in any conflict attempt to impose my authority on yours. "Freedom" and "God" and other such terms name the transcendent, but since the authority to which *I* defer is adequate to the transcendent, the authority to which *you* defer must not be. My freedom is Freedom, and my god is God.

One ill consequence of box 3 is that the untempered self-interest advocated by Machiavelli fails the Kantian test of universalizability and of complementarity of means and end. Only one person at a time can be *successful* at exempting himself (the masculine pronoun here, to reflect Machiavelli's gender assumptions). Monopoly, in business or in government, benefits one and harms all the rest.

The point is this. "Box four thinking" is the most to be admired, but also the hardest to achieve and sustain. As the only quadrant that legitimates civil disobedience (obeying, for instance, obligations imposed by Justice rather than those enforced by a justice system, when the latter contradicts the former), box four is the box that accommodates our most revered historical figures (Socrates, Jesus, Gandhi, Martin Luther King, et al.) and even our most revered fictional *characters* (e.g., Antigone, Cordelia). All who manage it are worthy of study and emulation. My case for the relevance of Fray Luis's poetry is that, as indicated by his life, Fray Luis achieved box four: he recognized the ultimacy of transcendence, as evident in his life of devotion, but he did not defer to authority as if it were final, as evident in his defiance of, and imprisonment by, his inquisitors. His poetry, like his life, reflects this important and difficult conceptual achievement. His poetry is not valuable because people are still reading it more than four centuries after its composition; people are still reading it because it is valuable. The poetry of Fray Luis rewards our attention in the same way that, say, Socrates' conversations (as presented by Plato) do: by elucidating and recommending box four.

2. HOW THESE POEMS WORK

Fray Luis draws much of the imagery and language for his poems from the Christian culture of his time and place, but does so, I contend, as an expression of the culture-independent paradox that "box four thinking" in any time and place accepts as its condition: we humans are mortal, yet capable of awareness whose limits extend forward and backward, well beyond the current moment and even beyond the duration of our own lives; we are material, yet imbued with consciousness, self-consciousness, and perception; we are capable not only of response to stimuli, but of such consciousness-dependent states and actions as hope, despair, decision; we can affiliate (at scales from a couple to a transnational organization), yet our inclusions are also exclusions, so that our affiliations create strife even as they create community; this life is everything and nothing. Box four thinking recognizes that, in Simone Weil's elegant formulation, "We know by means of our intelligence that what the intelligence does not comprehend is more real than what it does comprehend."[22] This paradoxical condition calls for *apposition*, in at least four domains, with vehicles of

22. Weil, *Gravity and Grace*, 182.

apposition proper to each domain. Again, a chart gives a way of condensing the comparison:

domain	metaphysical	ethical	practical	formal
appositional tenor	situation	ideal	practice	device
appositional vehicle	likeness	adequation	mimesis	repetition
methodology	resemble	live up to	imitate	repeat
metaphor	reflection/ image	harmony	approximation	replication
truth criterion	correspon-dence	consonance	congruity	coherence
aspect of humanity	what we are	what we might be	what we do	how we mean

The governing domain is the metaphysical: "transcendent" and "immanent" are themselves metaphysical terms. The very drawing of the distinction (whether or not the terms refer to anything "real") is normative: the distinction is a hierarchization. In Fray Luis's time and place, the distinction was drawn in terms of the Biblical theme, introduced in the creation narrative in Genesis, that humans are made in God's image. This way of drawing the distinction still has currency for many people. What I want to observe about it here, though, is that its "truth," the aspect of its meaning that is susceptible to other formulations as well, is that though we humans be immanent, yet we bear likeness to the transcendent (or, more forcefully, our being *is* likeness to the transcendent).

I call the metaphysical the governing domain because the others depend on and respond to it. It presents as a fact, but it entails value. (As at least some other facts do, also. For example: Humans derive their energy from food. Various values depend on and respond to that fact: e.g., I have an obligation to feed my family only because humans derive their energy from food. If we humans did not need food, I would have no obligation to feed my family.) This is why the division is so deep between boxes 1 and 3, on the one hand, and boxes 2 and 4, on the other: who we are, what we ought to do, and how we ought to treat one another, each is radically different if there is *not* a distinction between the transcendent and the immanent than if there *is* such a distinction. It is also why even the division between boxes 2 and 4 is deep. The answer to the question *Can we* resolve *the distinction between the transcendent and the immanent?* is another fact that entails value, so one who answers "yes" (enters box 2) pretends a different identity and embraces different obligations from one who answers "no" (thus entering box 4).

Our metaphysical situation imposes on us an ethical ideal. Insofar as likeness admits of degree, the metaphysical situation of bearing likeness to the transcendent will entail that our ideal be to bear ever *more* likeness to the transcendent, that we seek to adequate ourselves to the transcendent. Or, again in the terms that would have been most familiar for Fray Luis, our being made in the image of God will entail that we harmonize ourselves with that image. If what we are corresponds to the transcendent, then what we might be is consonant with it.

Similarly, in the domain of the practical, the appositional tenor and vehicle follow from the metaphysical. If our ideal must be to live up to the transcendent, then our practice must be to imitate it. Our practice will be mimetic. (As per Aristotle's practical advice that if I wish to be a flute player I imitate flute players: begin doing the things flute players do.) Through such mimesis we will approximate the transcendent. In the language of being made in the image of God, we will seek to make ourselves an ever more accurate approximation of what we are an image of.

Which brings us to the formal domain, the domain of signification and communication, and thus the primary realm of poetry. Here, repetition is the appositional vehicle, the corollary of the vehicles of the other domains: likening the immanent to the transcendent, adequating the real to the ideal, imitating our perfect selves in our flawed selves. Repetition is why meaning is meaningful. To borrow from Wendell Berry a capsule statement about the formal: "By its formal integrity a poem reminds us of the formal integrity of other works, creatures, and structures of the world.... Thus the poet affirms and collaborates in the formality of the Creation."[23]

Repetition as an appositional vehicle in the formal domain is not unique to Fray Luis, of course, or even to poetry. In prayer, for example, repetition is regarded by many as efficacious, as in repetition of such received prayers in Catholicism as the "Hail Mary" or the "Our Father." Similarly, meditation often includes, or is regarded as being induced by, repetition, such as the repetition of the syllable *om*. In reference to religious worship, to describe a form of worship as "liturgical" is to note the prevalence in it of structuring repetition.

As an example of repetition with particular relevance to Fray Luis, the Biblical Psalms, many of which Fray Luis himself translated, are structured by repetition. The first few lines of Psalm 100 illustrate the point: "Make a joyful noise to the Lord, all the earth. / Worship the Lord with gladness; /come into his presence with singing. // Know that the Lord is God. / It is he that made us, and we are his; / we are his people, and the sheep of his pasture" (Psalm 100: 1–3, New Revised Standard Version). Repetition occurs at various levels: within lines, elements are repeated, such as the idea that we are the Lord's people, repeated as our being the sheep of his pasture; repetition also takes place *as* lines, as when the imperative to worship is given in line 2 and repeated in line 3; and even at the level of the stanza, the structure of declaration followed by amplification is repeated. This kind of repetition exemplifies, according to G. B. Caird, "the paratactical style in which [logical] connections are implicit and taken for granted."[24] Such repetition allowed the Psalmist to "set two ideas side by side and allow the one to qualify the other without bothering to spell out in detail the relation between them,"[25] with conceptual and cultural effects: "Paratactical thinking enabled the ancient Hebrew to set in close

23. Berry, *What Are*, 89.

24. Caird, *The Language*, 118.

25. Caird, *The Language*, 118.

proximity two different, and even apparently contradictory, senses of a word, without the discomfort felt by the modern reader."[26]

The form of repetition employed by the Psalms is not the only form available, though, nor is juxtaposition of apparently contradictory ideas the only possible effect of repetition. Metaphor is a form of repetition. My love's being like a red, red rose doubles her: she is in/as herself and in/as the rose. Representation of any kind is, as the word itself indicates, a form of repetition. And repetition need not be transitive to realize the formal aspect of ourselves: repetition need not be repetition *of the transcendent* in order to replicate, to cohere with, the transcendent. Music, for instance, the most purely formal of our formal constructions, does not cohere with the transcendent by repeating the transcendent but by repeating notes from a scale. Similarly, poetry repeats sounds, words, lines, rhythmic patterns, and so on.

Insofar, then, as Fray Luis's poetry is the embodiment in the formal domain of the metaphysical condition of humanity as understood in box four thinking (just as his vocation embodies that metaphysical condition in the practical domain, and his imprisonment in the ethical domain), we would expect it to employ as its appositional vehicle repetition. It does exactly that. Consider as an example Luis's poem "Life Apart." Besides the most obvious forms of repetition (such as the repeated stanza form, itself a pattern of repeated sounds and rhythms), there is in this poem an extraordinary amount of lexical repetition. The original poem, "Vida retirada," employs a striking number of word repetitions and word plays. Not one of the seventeen stanzas fails to repeat at least one word that also appears in another stanza. By my count, twenty-seven different words are repeated, in a poem of only eighty-five lines:

árboles	el passo entre los árboles torciendo (52)
	los árboles menea / con un manso ruïdo (58–9)

26. Caird, *The Language*, 119.

bastar	de amable paz bien abastada (72) me baste (73)
cantar	No cura si la fama / canta con voz su nombre pregonera (11–12) Despiértenme las aves / con su cantar sabroso no aprendido (31–2) tendido yo a la sombra esté cantando (80)
cielo	gozar quiero del bien que devo al cielo (37) al cielo suena / confusa vozería (68–9)
confiar	Ténganse su tesoro / los que de un falso leño se confían (61) no es mío ver el lloro / de los que desconfían (63–4)
cuidado	con ansias vivas, con mortal cuidado (20) no los cuidados graves / de que es siempre seguido (33–4)
cura	No cura si la fama / canta con voz su nombre pregonera (11–12) ni cura si encarama / la lengua lisonjera (13–14)
día	un día puro, alegre, libre quiero (27) en ciega noche el claro día / se torna (67–8)
esperança	libre de amor, de zelo, / de odio, de esperanças, de rezelo (39–40) ya muestra en esperança el fruto cierto (45)
flor	de bella flor cubierto (44) y con diversas flores va esparciendo (55)

huerto	por mi mano plantado tengo un huerto (42) El ayre el huerto orea (56)
huir	la del que huye el mundanal ruïdo (2) huyo de aqueste mar tempestuoso (25)
libre	un día puro, alegre, libre quiero (27) libre de amor, de zelo (39)
mar	huyo de aqueste mar tempestuoso (25) y la mar enriquecen a porfía (70) sea de quien la mar no teme ayrada (75)
menear	los árboles menea / con un manso ruïdo (58–9) del plectro sabiamente meneado (85)
monte	¡O monte, o fuente, o río! (21) Del monte en la ladera (41)
oro	que del oro y del cetro pone olvido (60) y la baxilla / de fino oro labrada (73–4)
passar	el passo entre los árboles torciendo (52) el suelo, de passada (53)
porfíar	quando el cierço y el ábrego porfían (65) y la mar enriquecen a porfía (70)
querer	un día puro, alegre, libre quiero (27) no quiero ver el zeño (28) Vivir quiero conmigo (36) gozar quiero del bien que devo al cielo (37)
romper	roto casi el navío (23) Un no rompido sueño (26)

ruïdo	la del que huye el mundanal ruïdo (2) los árboles menea / con un manso ruïdo (58–9)
sabio	los pocos sabios que en el mundo han sido (5) fabricado / del sabio moro, en jaspes sustentado (9–10) del plectro sabiamente meneado (85)
seguir	y sigue la escondida / senda (3–4) no los cuidados graves / de que es siempre seguido (33–4)
sombra	tendido yo a la sombra esté cantando (80) A la sombra tendido (81)
tender	tendido yo a la sombra esté cantando (80) A la sombra tendido (81)
ver	no quiero ver el zeño (28) Y como codiciosa / por ver y acrecentar su hermosura (46–7) de verdura vistiendo (54) no es mío ver el lloro (63)
vivir	¡Qué descansada vida (1) con ansias vivas, con mortal cuidado (20) Vivir quiero conmigo (36)

This list does not include repetition-based forms of word play, such as use of synonyms (e.g., two words for fountain/spring: *fuente* in line 21 and *fontana* in line 49) or compoundings (e.g., *oro* (60) / *tesoro* (61), or *zelo* (39) / *rezelo* (40)).

What does such a quantity of lexical repetition *do*? Joseph Brodsky defines a poet as "someone for whom every word is not the end but the beginning of a thought; someone who, having uttered *rai* ('paradise') or *tot svet* ('next world'), must mentally take the subsequent step of finding a rhyme for it. Thus *krai* ('edge/realm') and *otsvet* ('reflection') emerge, and the existence of those whose life has ended is prolonged"[27]: rhyme confers a kind of immortality. My assertion is not identical to Brodsky's, but I take it as related: repetitions reiterate in the formal domain the metaphysical situation, and thus the most elemental identity, of humans. To take only the first instance on the list, *arbol* (tree), Fray Luis is a poet who, seeing spring water "winding its way among the trees," whose roots, silent and fixed in place, draw upon the water to nourish the tree, must see again. Thus does "each tree stirs / with soothing noises" emerge, noting the leaves, *not* silent and *not* immobile, that return nourishment to the tree's surroundings, and the identity of humans, our relationship to immanence and to transcendence, is enacted, and clarified.

3. ABOUT THIS EDITION

It is an irony (or paradox, or tragedy) of translation that the feature of the original poems on which I have just meditated at such length, repetition, cannot be replicated — repeated — in translation. Take, for one example, the repetition of *sabio*. In Willis Barnstone's translation, the instances of *sabio* become three different and etymologically unrelated English words: *wise*, *skilled*, and *artfully*. Similarly, in my translation, the three instances of *sabio* become three different and etymologically unrelated English words: *wise*, *deft*, and *expertly*. I can only hope, appealing to the definition, sometimes attributed to Robert Frost, of poetry as "what is lost in translation," that the very loss of the lexical repetition in the original is a gesture toward "the poetry of the poetry."

I have argued for the poetry of Fray Luis as *living* and *relevant*, bearing on our contemporary lives and values and self-understanding, not as having primarily historical and archival

27. Brodsky, *Less Than One*, 265.

value. Similarly, I have used as my basis for arranging the poems in relation to one another a principle other than the artifactual. Instead of attempting to recuperate and follow the order of their first presentation, I have tried to discern relationships between the poems, and commonalities across them, that suggest an order inherent in them, an order that puts them into logical sequence so that each feels connected to the one before it and the one after it, and so that the whole exceeds the sum of its parts.

In so arranging the poems I assert nothing about Fray Luis's intentionality. I claim only that the order is implicit in the poems, that it is one logic of relationship available to the poems through their various individual characters. Any poet gathering her poems into a collection does the same. Poems are complex entities, and a gathering of several such complex entities will lend itself to various arrangements, each with its own logic and its own effects on the individual poems. (I might arrange my poems chronologically in order of their composition, an arrangement that would emphasize their each reflecting a stage in one person's thinking or experience; I might cluster them into birth, death, and rebirth poems, an arrangement that would emphasize their framing of human experience within a mythic narrative; and so on.) In arranging these poems as I have, I do not claim that Fray Luis did choose, or that he would have chosen, this arrangement, only that it is an arrangement with an explicable logic, an arrangement that draws on, and draws out, aspects of the poems an awareness of which enriches the reading of them.

That is to say: this is a reader's edition, rather than a scholar's edition, of the poems. My purpose has not been to advance knowledge about Fray Luis, but to facilitate access to his poems and the wisdom they offer.

I have placed "Vida Retirada" at the very center, as the twelfth of the twenty-three poems: eleven precede it, eleven follow it. (At the risk of tedium, I reiterate that in doing so I do not assert that Fray Luis thought this poem was central, only that I — concurring in this case with a tradition that anthologizes this poem more often than any other by Fray Luis — regard it as central.) I have placed "In the Highest Sphere" at the beginning because it opens with a question about when we will be *metaphorically* free from imprisonment, and "On Release from Prison" last because it is a reflection occasioned by Fray Luis's *literal* freedom from imprisonment. The rest of the poems are arranged by the organizing tensions of each, with poems focused on "external" contextual conditions earlier, and poems focused on "internal" conditions later. The progression, in other words, is from how things are in the world to how things are within me.

From a scholarly point of view, the arrangement of the poems is interventionist: I have made no attempt to discover an original order actually imposed by Fray Luis, or to postulate an original order intended by him, nor have I deferred to any one of the various arrangements made by prior editions. Instead, I have sought to discover in the poems themselves relationships of continuity across poems, and transitions from one poem to another, that create a viable path for a reader. (An appendix following this introduction compares my ordering to that of other representative editions.)

This Introduction begins by making a case for the importance and relevance of Fray Luis's poetry; let me also give a rationale for a new translation of them. There are, after all, various translations of individual poems by Fray Luis into English. For example, the Edith Grossman *Golden Age* anthology and the J. M. Cohen *Penguin Book of Spanish Verse*, cited above, each contains four poems by Fray Luis. And though there is, to my knowledge, only one complete edition of all of Fray Luis's poetry in English translation, Willis Barnstone's *The Unknown Light*, it is a modern edition (1979), by a very accomplished and prolific translator. Why a new translation, then, from a translator not nearly so distinguished as Grossman, Cohen, or Barnstone? First, the poems have an integrity as a group, not only as separate, individual poems, so a complete edition of all twenty-three poems is called for, which leaves the Cohen and Grossman individual translations (and their many siblings in numerous anthologies), for all their virtues, wanting completion. Barnstone's edition is complete in one sense, namely that all twenty-three original poems are presented, but his edition has its own version of incompleteness: sixteen of the poems, under the heading "Poems," are presented in verse translation, but the remaining seven poems, under the heading "Appendix: Other Poems," are presented in prose translation. The present edition is, then, to my knowledge, the only volume in print that includes verse translations of all twenty-three poems by Fray Luis into English, all translated by the same hand. Even if no one translation from this edition can compete with, say, Grossman's translation of the same poem, the whole edition nevertheless stands as the first of its kind, and fills a longstanding void. Besides, there can never be too many translations of a valuable original (as per T. S. Eliot's reminder that there is no competition).

Most of the original poems employ Fray Luis's favorite verse form, "la lira," a five-line stanza he adopted from Garcilaso, who adopted it from the Italian poetry of Tasso, who was attempting to recreate the metrical forms of Horace. Most Spanish-language poetry uses syllabic lineation: in the lira, the lines have, respectively, 7, 11, 7, 7, and 11 syllables. It is rhymed aBabB (the small letters designate assonantal rhyme and capitals consonantal rhyme). I have cheated. For seven-syllable lines, I substitute a line with two heavy accents, and for the eleven-syllable lines a line with four heavy accents; but I allow the number of syllables per line to vary widely. I also play fast and loose with rhyme, maintaining only the pattern of rhyming first line with third, and second with fourth and fifth, but *not* maintaining the assonantal/consonantal distinction. My resorting to sometimes very slant rhyme (e.g. state/gilt/deft) is dictated by need rather than by principle, a capitulation for which I plead as my excuse the greater difficulty of rhyming in English than in Spanish.

Formally, then, I have followed rules that *evoke* those Fray Luis was following, but also draw on formal traditions in English-language poetry, and (more importantly) that have the flexibility to allow me, while nodding to his attention to rhyme and meter, to honor as far as possible his natural word order and deliberate word choice. That word choice *was* deliberate: it *mattered* to Fray

Luis. He believed, as Colin Thompson puts it, not in an accidental relationship between, but in an "ideal union of," word and meaning; for him, "the word is a spiritual reality, which enables the individual to participate in all the variety of creation, and it in him."[28]

Fray Luis's deliberate word choice notwithstanding, there are variations across the several modern Spanish editions of the poems. The transmission history of the poems is problematic: the poems were not published until forty years after the poet's death, and even then in dubious form; it is not always clear which of the poems attributed to Fray Luis he actually wrote; spurious versions circulated even during his lifetime; and so on. Even after the monumental editorial labor of Father Antolín Merino in the early 1800s, which went a long way toward establishing a canon and standardizing versions, some variations persist. Most are relatively minor. In some cases, these are simple editorial predilections, such as whether or not to modernize spelling. In a few cases, there are questions about whether whole stanzas do or do not belong in the poem. The great majority are on the order of the variations across these presentations of the sixth stanza of "Vida Retirada" in various editions, here collated.

1=Cuevas; 2=Blecua; 3=Durán y Atlee; 4= Tesán;
5=García; 6=Vega; 7=Barnstone

1 & 2	Un no rompido sueño,
3	Un no rompido sueño,
4	Un no rompido sueño,
5	Un no rompido sueño,
6 & 7	Un no rompido sueño,

un día puro, alegre, libre quiero;
un día puro, alegre, libre quiero;
un día puro, alegre, libre, quiero;
un día puro, alegre, libre, quiero;
un día puro, alegre, libre quiero;

28. Thompson, *The Strife of Tongues*, 177.

no quiero ver el zeño
no quiero ver el ceño
no quiero ver el ceño
no quiero ver el ceño
no quiero ver el ceño

vanamente severo
vanamente severo
vanamente severo
vanamente severo
vanamente severo

de a quien la sangre ensalça, o el dinero.
de a quien la sangre ensalza, o el dinero.
de a quien la sangre ensalza o el dinero.
de a quien la sangre ensalza o el dinero.
del que la sangre sube o el dinero.

In this stanza, only two of the five lines are identical in all the editions, yet only the last line has a "major" variation. Cuevas and Blecua match one another throughout, as do Vega and Barnstone (though Cuevas/Blecua does not match Vega/Barnstone). Otherwise, each edition's version differs in some way from all the rest. This stanza is, in that way, a typical one. In the present edition, I have not followed any one editor's decisions consistently, though I have hewn more closely to Cuevas' original-spelling edition than to modernized-spelling editions.

In another regard, I have intervened actively. Fray Luis himself did not give titles to the poems, though all modern editions do give titles. Some titles are consistent across editions, others are not. Here, too, I have not followed any one edition consistently, but have tried to choose the most "informative" title available for the Spanish poem. More importantly, for the translations I have exaggerated the tradition of appending titles, by departing in several cases from the available Spanish titles. I have done so primarily for clarity: several of the poems bear titles that are dedications (e.g., "To Don Pedro Portocarrero"), and some of those are used for more than one poem. I have relegated dedicatory titles to subtitles, and invented a new title, in each case one unique to the poem.

4. ONE PATH THROUGH THE POEMS

If the poems work by apposition, as I have argued in §2 above, they also work by opposition. In a discussion of one of Fray Luis's prose works, Colin P. Thompson notes that antitheses (in this case, two in particular, real/false and just/unjust) "are not merely rhetorical flourishes." They are integral to the work, expressing in this case "the new understanding Fray Luis reached in the midst of his tribulations, that God could take what in human terms is false and unjust and use it for a just and proper end."[29] Such oppositions or antitheses are integral to the poems no less than to the prose works, and I have taken them as a primary determinant of the sequence in which I present the poems here.

I have placed "In the Highest Sphere" first because it begins with the speaker in prison, thus creating, in conjunction with the placing of "On Release from Prison" last, a movement from imprisonment to release, which the poems collectively suggest was central to Fray Luis's narrative of his own life, and crucial to his broader understanding of how things are, and how they might be, for us as humans. But I place "In the Highest Sphere" first also because it introduces the opposition *cielo/tierra* (heaven/earth), which recurs frequently in the poems, and gives Fray Luis a "cosmic map" for his valuations. "Almost with Wings" also employs the opposition *cielo/tierra*, but adds to it *noche/dia* (night/day), another opposition that Fray Luis appeals to often in the poems. If *cielo/tierra* creates a spatial field on which to map valuations, *noche/dia* creates a temporal field.

29. Thompson, *The Strife of Tongues*, 73.

The two fields identified in the first two poems are then supplemented in the second two. "Song for the Birth of a Noble Daughter" uses the opposition *alto/baxo* (high/low), qualities that correlate with *cielo/tierra*, and "Quiet Night" uses the opposition *reluciente/escura* (luminous/dark), qualities that correlate with *noche/dia*. "On the Ascension" adds another metaphor to the array of metaphors used in the poems, by contrasting *mar turbado* (stormy sea) with *el puerto* (port). "To Our Lady" employs a related contrast, between being *de nubes rodeado* (enveloped by clouds) and having *en mar tempestuoso clara guía* (on a tempestuous sea a clear guide).

"Heavenly Dwelling" opposes *traspasar* (to go through), purposive and directional movement, to *vagar* (to wander), aimless, drifting movement, and also contrasts *fértil suelo* (fertile soil) to *prisión* (prison). "Respite After the Storm" employs the opposition of *trabajar perdido* (wasted or futile labor) to *reposo dulce* (sweet repose), an opposition related to the contrast in "Another Mode" between *reposo* (rest) and *despertar* (to wake). "Of Magdalene: To a Woman Past Her Youth" and "The Prophecy of the Tajo" also use related oppositions: "Of Magdalene" contrasts the actions *laviar* and *limpiar* (to wash, to clean) with the materials on which they act, *polvo* and *suelo* (dust and dirt); "The Prophecy of the Tajo" contrasts the action *tender* (to lay out or arrange) with the condition it contests, *desordena* (messy, untidy).

The oppositions noted so far, in the first 11 poems, have tended to be "external"; that is, to be things or actions in the world, visible or tangible to all. The oppositions that follow, in the last 11 poems, tend to be "internal"; that is, to be conditions or experiences that are properties of persons rather than of the world. I have placed "Vida retirada" at the exact center, between the two groups, because it so resolutely coordinates external with internal, and makes use, explicitly or implicitly, of so many of the contrasts identified by the other poems.

"To Santiago" contrasts *cantar* (to sing) with *sufrir* (to suffer), and "To an Absent Friend" contrasts *paz* (peace) with *vencer* (to conquer). "Your Ascent" opposes *recoger* (to pick up, gather in) to *romper* (to break). The pattern is clear, that Fray Luis is interested in distinguishing that which is desirable and good from that which is undesirable and bad, in the world, in what we do, and in our conditions and feelings.

In "With a Hundred Voices, With Swift Flight," the contrast is between *el falso engaño* (false deceit) and *la verdad* (truth), which prepares for the contrast in "The Sirens" between *engañar* (to deceive) and *fies* (faith). Even if the theme of "Against an Avaricious Judge" is not more subtle than that of "The Sirens," the operative contrast is: the action of *comprar* and *vender* (synonyms, both meaning to sell) versus the conditions of *esperanza* and *verdad* (hope and truth, respectively).

Each of the next three poems deploys an opposition of conditions of a person: *riqueza/pobre* (rich/poor) in "Of Avarice," *contento/triste* (happy/sad) in "Absurd Hopes," and *muerta/vida* (dead/living) in "For All Saints." "Of Moderation and Constancy" emphasizes a sequenced opposition, *despedazar* (to cut into pieces, to pull apart) versus *tornar* (to return). Finally, "On Release from Prison" returns to the prison motif introduced in the poem I placed first, "In the Highest Sphere," contrasting *cárcel* (prison) with *el campo deleytoso* (delightful field).

My hope for this arrangement of the poems is that it brings to the surface certain resonances between the poems, creating a call and response that the reader will find a welcoming and evocative aspect of the reading, and that the arrangement, by embodying one arc of the poems, will make the movement from poem to poem illuminating, too, just as is the lingering in any given poem.

1. In the Highest Sphere

THIS POEM BEGINS WITH the speaker in prison, a metaphor that Fray Luis uses frequently, and that relates to his lived experience. Colin P. Thompson suggests that Fray Luis's use of the prison metaphor is not only frequent, but also broad, operating, like "metaphor in general, to express in as vivid and concrete a way as possible concepts which belong to the realms of philosophy and theology and to the interpretations these disciplines give to the puzzles of human experience."[1]

In this poem, the contrast between mortal imprisonment and spiritual freedom is established in part by the echoes in it of two familiar Biblical passages. Throughout the poem, but especially in the third through the seventh stanzas, Fray Luis evokes God's reply to Job out of the whirlwind: "Then the Lord answered Job out of the whirlwind: / 'Who is this that darkens counsel by words without knowledge? / Gird up your loins like a man, / I will question you, and you shall declare to me. // 'Where were you when I laid the foundation of the earth? / Tell me, if you have understanding. / Who determined its measurements—surely you know! / Or who stretched the line upon it? / On what were its bases sunk, / or who laid its cornerstone / when the morning stars sang together / and all the heavenly beings shouted for joy?"[2]

The echo of that reminder of the limits of human understanding is framed by the echo, introduced in Luis's second stanza, of the

1. Thompson, *The Strife of Tongues*, 79.

2. Job 38: 1–7, New Revised Standard Version.

expectation, formulated in Paul's First Letter to the Corinthians, that our understanding will deepen in the future: "For we know only in part, and we prophesy only in part; but when the complete comes, the partial will come to an end.... For now we see in a mirror, dimly, but then we will see face to face. Now I know only in part; then I will know fully, even as I have been fully known."[3]

In this way, Luis signals that he shares Job's recognition of the severe limits of his mortal state, but also signals that he shares Paul's hope for a glorious future state.

3. I Cor. 13: 9–12, New Revised Standard Version.

A FELIPE RUIZ

¿Quándo será que pueda
libre desta prisión bolar al cielo,
Felipe, y en la rueda
que huye más del suelo
contemplar la verdad pura sin duelo?
Allí, a mi vida junto,
en luz resplandeciente convertido,
veré distinto y junto
lo que es y lo que ha sido,
y su principio propio y ascondido.
Entonces veré cómo
la soberana mano echó el cimiento
tan a nivel y plomo,
do estable y firme assiento
possee el pesadíssimo elemento.
Veré las inmortales
colunas, do la tierra está fundada;
las lindes y señales
con que a la mar hinchada
la Providencia tiene aprisionada;
por qué tiembla la tierra;
por qué las hondas mares se embravecen;
dó sale a mover guerra
el cierço, y por qué crecen
las aguas del océano y descrecen;
de dó manan las fuentes;
quién ceba y quién bastece de los ríos
las perpetuas corrientes;
de los elados fríos
veré las causas, y de los estíos;
las soberanas aguas

IN THE HIGHEST SPHERE

To Felipe Ruiz

When will I, free
from this prison, be able to fly to heaven,
Felipe, and in the sphere
farthest from this one
contemplate truth untainted by pain?
There, finally at one
with my life, converted to light, glorious,
I will see as one
what is and what was,
the original and actual and mysterious.
I'll be able to tell
how the sovereign hand laid the cement
plumb and level,
a stable, secure seat
for even the heaviest element.
I will see the immortal
columns on which the earth is founded;
the boundaries and signals
stopping the swollen flood
that Providence keeps imprisoned;
why earth quakes;
why the oceans are tempestuous;
why the north wind attacks,
and why the waters
of the deep ocean increase and decrease;
why springs emanate;
who fills and replenishes the rivers
with a constant current;
of frozen glaciers
I will see the causes, and of hot summers;
who is sustaining

del ayre en la región quién las sostiene;
de los rayos las fraguas;
dó los tesoros tiene
de nieve Dios, y el trueno dónde viene.
    ¿No ves quando acontece
turbarse el ayre todo en el verano?
El día se enegrece,
sopla el gallego insano
y sube hasta el cielo el polvo vano;
    y entre las nubes mueve
su carro Dios ligero y reluciente;
horrible son conmueve,
relumbra fuego ardiente,
treme la tierra, humíllase la gente;
    la lluvia baña el techo;
invían largos ríos los collados;
su trabajo deshecho,
los campos anegados
miran los labradores espantados.
    Y de allí levantado,
veré los movimientos celestiales,
ansí el arrebatado,
como los naturales;
las causas de los hados, las señales.
    Quién rige las estrellas
veré, y quién las enciende con hermosas
y eficazes centellas;
por qué están las dos Osas
de bañarse en la mar siempre medrosas.
    Veré este fuego eterno,
fuente de vida y luz, dó se mantiene,
y por qué en el hibierno
tan presuroso viene;

the waters that reign over the air;
the bolts of lightning;
where God keeps his store
of snow, and where it comes from, the thunder.
    Have you not seen
in spring how the whole atmosphere stirs?
The day darkens,
the west wind blows,
and vain dust rises into the skies;
    God's chariot dashes
to and fro, luminous, among the clouds;
hot fire flashes,
there's an awful sound,
earth trembles, people are cowed;
    rain washes the roof;
the hills send sudden rivers down;
their fields engulfed,
their work undone,
the terrified farmers look on.
    There lifting my gaze,
I will see the celestial movements,
the wanderers and those
on courses that are fixed,
the causes and signs of our fates.
    Who rules the stars
I will see, who confers influence on
their beautiful glimmers;
why, fearing immersion,
the two Bears always avoid the ocean.
    I will see the eternal fire,
fountain of life and light, where it waits;
and why in winter
it so quickly departs,

quién en las noches largas le detiene.
    Veré sin movimiento,
en la más alta esfera, las moradas
del gozo y del contento,
de oro y luz labradas,
de espíritus dichosos habitadas.

who holds it back through the long nights.
    In the highest sphere
I will see the unmoved mover, the abode
of joy and pleasure,
of golden, refined
light, of spirits secure and blessed.

2. Almost with Wings

"Almost with Wings" prepares the reader for a number of poems that will follow, especially "Quiet Night" and "Another Mode." All three poems express the desire to overcome the celestial barrier between earth and heaven, but subtle differences reveal Luis's employment of a received equivalence (*el cielo* names both the sky and heaven) as a vehicle for restless inquiry. "Quiet Night" looks up and sees "the great concert / of these resplendencies eternal." The speaker observes that the stars, their permanence and order and beauty, figure the divine. As if one were looking not *at* them but *through* them, they reveal "a light clear and pure / that never darkens," that illuminates this otherwise dark world. If in "Quiet Night" the organ of perception is the eye, in "Another Mode" it is the ear. The speaker hears music, and so richly does it resonate with the heavenly harmony that the speaker's soul is transported to heaven. In "Almost with Wings," the organ of perception is the mind, which is able to recognize Virtue, and thus guide the addressee and subject of the poem, Luis's friend Pedro Portocarrero, across the "great space" from earthly to heavenly conditions.

In "Quiet Night" the apposition (becoming *like* the ideal, instead of contrasting to it) occurs in, and is perceptible as, the stars. In "Another Mode" the apposition is provoked by earthly music and occurs as harmony. In "Almost with Wings" the apposition is occasioned by heavenly Virtue and occurs as elevation and survey: the mountaintop vista.

Fray Luis's skillful use of repetition is beautifully illustrated here in the second stanza. To realize its depiction of Portocarrero as an heroic Christian, the poem makes a three-way analogy between Portocarrero, heroes from classical mythology, and heroes from Spanish myth/history. In the second stanza, rather than calling Heracles (Hercules) by his most familiar name, Luis calls him by the name given him at birth, Alcides, the first two syllables of which he repeats three lines later, as "al Cid," to connect the Greek hero Heracles with the Cid, one of the most important Spanish heroes.

A DON PEDRO PORTOCARRERO

Virtud, hija del cielo,
la más ilustre empresa de la vida,
en el escuro suelo
luz tarde conocida,
senda que guía al bien, poco seguida.
Tú dende la hoguera
al cielo levantaste al fuerte Alcides;
tú en la más alta esfera
con las estrellas mides
al Cid, clara victoria de mil lides.
Por ti el passo desvía
de la profunda noche, y resplandece
muy más qu'el claro día
de Leda el parto, y crece
el Córdoba a las nubes y florece.
Y por tu senda agora
traspassa luengo espacio con ligero
pie y ala boladora
el gran Portocarrero,
osado de ocupar el bien primero.
Del vulgo se descuesta.
Hollando sobre el oro, firme aspira
a lo alto de la cuesta.
Ni vïolencia de ira,
ni blando y dulce engaño le retira.
Ni mueve más ligera,
ni más igual divide por derecha
el ayre y fiel carrera,
o la traciana flecha
o la bola tudesca un fuego hecha.
En pueblo inculto y duro

ALMOST WITH WINGS

To Don Pedro Portocarrero

Virtue, heaven's daughter,
of life's labors the most illustrious,
dark soil's wonder
at the light of dusk,
less-taken road that leads to goodness.
Up from the fire
to heaven you raised strong Alcides;
in the highest sphere
you test by the stars
the Cid's thousand brilliant victories.
To you the way
detours around deep night, and splendors
bright as the birthday
of Leda, and towers
like Córdoba to the clouds, where it flowers.
On the way to you now,
with light foot he crosses the great space,
noble Portocarrero,
with wings almost,
daring to go before the rest.
He keeps apart
from the crowd. He walks on gold, yearns
for the hilltop, not
distracted by violence
and anger, not by soft, sweet illusions.
They could not split the air
more justly, nor move more swiftly, nor so
straightly career,
not the Thracian arrow,
not the fiery Teutonic cannon salvo.
Even the hardest, coarsest

induce poderoso igual costumbre,
y, do se muestra escuro
el cielo, enciende lumbre,
valiente a ilustrar más alta cumbre.
    Dichosos los que baña
el Miño, los que el mar monstruoso cierra,
dende la fiel montaña
hasta el fin de la tierra,
los que desprecia de Eume la alta sierra.

people it can raise to a level of discernment,
and even the darkest
sky it can give light
strong enough to illuminate the mountain's height.
    Happy are those who
bathe in the Miño, those from the Cordillera
Cantábrica to
Finisterre,
who face the monster-swarmed sea from Eume's sierra.

3. Song for the Birth of a Noble Daughter

To celebrate the birth of the daughter of the Marquis of Alcañices, this poem adopts the traditional form of a *genethliacon*, a type of poem David J. Hildner defines as "a circumstantial poem written for the birth or birthday of either a famous person or one who is dear to the poet. The Greek name refers not only to birth, but also to the horoscopes, prophecies and good wishes which accompany such an event, that is to say, an expression of the poetic speakers' expectations concerning the newborn's future."[1] Fray Luis fulfills the conventions of the form by populating the poem with Greek gods and goddesses (sometimes describing, rather than naming, the gods: "the god who rules the sixth orbit" is Jupiter, "the goddess who oversees the third" is Venus, and "the niggardly, envious old man" is Saturn).

But *only* fulfilling conventions, without also pushing against them, would not result in a satisfying poem, and Hildner points out a subtle way in which the poem is *un*conventional, noting that "throughout the poem there is an alternation of future indicative with subjunctive or imperative verbs."[2] Though that grammatical subtlety is not easy to capture accurately in translation, its effect comes through: Hildner points out that the alternation of verb tenses makes "the poem vacillate between a prediction and an

1. Hildner, *Poetry and Truth*, 147.
2. Hildner, *Poetry and Truth*, 149.

admonition to the baby girl about her future obligations."[3] This is most visible in the two stanzas toward the middle, in the first of which the daughter is assured by Apollo that Jupiter will give her "the glory / most fit for this terrestrial circle," but then immediately charges her with responsibility: "In exchange, you [should] tender / the eternal gifts of nobility, / honesty, high desire, / great generosity, / clear wisdom, faith full of purity."

In this way, the reach of the poem extends beyond its occasion: Doña Tomasina, the daughter whose birth the poem celebrates, becomes representative rather than exceptional. Her socially constructed "nobility" serves less to establish her difference from the rest of us than to stand for a nobility that Fray Luis sees as shared by all humans: we all are endowed by grace, rather than merit, with gifts (of life and intelligence and talents, even for those of us not born, like Doña Tomasina, into wealth), and thus responsible to enact grace ourselves.

3. Hildner, *Poetry and Truth*, 149.

CANCIÓN AL NACIMIENTO DE LA HIJA DEL MARQUÉS DE ALCAÑICES

Inspira nuevo canto,
Calíope, en mi pecho aqueste día,
que de los Borjas canto,
y Enríquez, la alegría
del rico don que el cielo les invía.
Hermoso sol luciente,
que el día das y llevas, rodeado
de luz resplandeciente
más de lo acostumbrado,
sal, y verás nacido tu traslado.
O, si te place agora
en la región contraria hazer manida,
detente allá en buen hora,
que con la luz nacida
podrá ser nuestra esfera esclarecida.
Alma divina, en belo
de femeniles miembros encerrada:
quando veniste al suelo,
robaste de passada
la celestial riquíssima morada.
Diéronte bien sin cuento,
con voluntad concorde y amorosa,
quien rige el movimiento
sexto, con la dïosa
de la tercera rueda poderosa.
De tu belleza rara
el embidioso viejo mal pagado,
torció el passo y la cara,
y el fiero Marte ayrado
el camino dexó desocupado.

SONG FOR THE BIRTH OF A NOBLE DAUGHTER

Today, Calliope,
inspire a new song in my breast,
a song of the families
Borja and Enriquez,
of the gift sent them by heaven's largesse.
Luminous sun
who ushers in the day, crowned
with even more than
your usual illumination,
come, witness the birth of your translation.
Or if it's your will
now to shine on the other side of the earth,
stay there a while,
that the light of her birth
be the sphere whose radiance we see with.
Divine soul, clothed with
the sheer drape of a feminine bearing,
when you came to earth
you stole in passing
the very richest celestial dwelling.
They endowed you well
with a will of measureless love and concord,
the god who rules
the sixth orbit,
and the goddess who oversees the third.
From your rare beauty
the niggardly, envious old man turned
his face away,
and even bold,
angry Mars left your path unobstructed.

Y el roxo y crespo Apolo
que, tus passos guiando, descendía
contigo al baxo polo,
la cítara hería,
y con divino canto ansí dezía:
— Deciende en punto bueno,
espíritu real, al cuerpo hermoso
que en el ilustre seno
te espera, deseoso
por dar a tu valor digno reposo.
Él te dará la gloria
que en el terreno cerco es más tenida:
de agüelos larga historia,
por quien la no undida
nave, por quien la España fue regida.
Tú dale, en cambio desto,
de los eternos bienes la nobleza,
deseo alto, honesto,
generosa grandeza,
claro saber, fe llena de pureza.
En su rostro se vean
de tu beldad sin par vivas señales;
los sus dos ojos sean
dos luzes inmortales,
que guíen al sumo bien a los mortales.
El cuerpo delicado,
como cristal lucido y transparente,
tu gracia y bien sagrado,
tu luz, tu continente,
a sus dichosos siglos represente.
La soberana agüela,
dechado de virtud y hermosura,
la tía, de quien buela

And the curly-haired
redhead, Apollo, who, guiding
your steps, descended
with you, vexing
his lyre, in divine strains sang:
— Descend to the right post,
true spirit, to the beautiful body whose
illustrious breast
awaits you, anxious
to give your valor dignified repose.
He'll give you the glory
most fit for this terrestrial circle:
a long history
of ancestors who ruled
Spain, and ruled the Ship Unsinkable.
In exchange, you tender
the eternal gifts of nobility,
honesty, high desire,
great generosity,
clear wisdom, faith full of purity.
On your face may one see
in your unrivalled beauty lively signs;
may your two eyes be
immortal beacons,
guides to the highest good for humans.
The delicate body,
like crystal lucid and transparent,
your grace and holy
virtue, your continence,
your light, your blessed centuries refracts.
Your royal forebear,
that paragon of virtue and of beauty;
your aunt, everywhere

la fama, en quien la dura
muerte mostró lo poco que el bien dura,
    con todas quantas precio
de gracia y de velleza ayan tenido,
serán por ti en desprecio
y puestas en olvido,
qual haze la verdad con lo fingido.
    ¡Ay, tristes; ay, dichosos
los ojos que te vieren! Huyan luego,
si fueren poderosos,
antes que prenda el fuego,
contra quien no valdrá ni oro ni ruego.
    Ilustre y tierna planta,
dulce gozo de tronco generoso,
creciendo, te levanta
a estado el más dichoso
de quantos dio ya el cielo venturoso.

acclaimed, but by
whom death proved good things transitory:
    though they possessed
all I prize of beauty and of grace,
yet theirs next
to yours looks worthless,
forgettable as the true renders the false.
    How happy sad eyes
will be when they see you! Even the mighty
the fire seizes,
so let them flee
what they cannot ward off by gold or by plea.
    Tender and lustrous,
of a generous trunk the sweet fruit:
its growth raises
you to that estate
heaven gives the happiest, the most blest.

4. Quiet Night

THIS POEM'S TITLE, "NOCHE serena," echoes the title of "La Noche oscura del alma" ("The Dark Night of the Soul"), the famous poem by Fray Luis's contemporary, St. John of the Cross, but Enrica Cancelliere distinguishes Fray Luis's employment of night as a metaphor from the more familiar employment in St. John of the Cross. The serene night of Fray Luis, Cancelliere says, "is not the same as the *dark night* of St. John, the night in which one goes to the depths and in which the subject is dispersed in effusiveness, without fear of the obscurity that is the same as very intense light, and without fear of being engulfed, because it is precisely this that one seeks. ¶ The night of Fray Luis, in contrast, is converted, in this way surpassing the night of torment, of anguish and of doubt, into the night of melancholy, the first stage of a cosmic Eros, that, across absence and desire, channels the luminosity, totally internal, implosive in the cosmos and in the subject, of the *Quiet Night*."[1]

To put Cancelliere's observation in another way, John's night is dark, but Luis's night is very bright: "here shines / a light clear and pure / that never darkens." Though the world and our mortal lives are "a prison, dark and dirty," full of "darkness and deception," in Luis's night the sky rather than the earth dominates: the moon gives light, and the stars and the visible planets (here personified as the gods who have lent them their names, Venus, Mars, Jupiter,

1. Cancelliere, "La celebración," 172, my translation.

and Saturn) display a "great concert" of "resplendencies eternal" that reveal "how low this dust lies."

NOCHE SERENA

Quando contemplo el cielo,
de innumerables luzes adornado,
y miro hazia el suelo
de noche rodeado,
en sueño y en olvido sepultado,
el amor y la pena
despiertan en mi pecho un ansia ardiente;
despiden larga vena
los ojos hechos fuente,
Oloarte, y digo al fin con voz doliente:
—Morada de grandeza,
templo de claridad y hermosura,
el alma, que a tu alteza
nació, ¿qué desventura
la tiene en esta cárcel baxa, escura?
¿Qué mortal desatino
de la verdad alexa assí el sentido,
que, de tu bien divino
olvidado, perdido
sigue la vana sombra, el bien fingido?
El hombre está entregado
al sueño, de su suerte no cuidando,
y con passo callado,
el cielo, bueltas dando,
las horas del vivir le va hurtando.
¡O, despertad, mortales!
¡Mirad con atención en vuestro daño!
Las almas inmortales,
hechas a bien tamaño,
¿podrán vivir de sombras y de engaño?
¡Ay, levantad los ojos

QUIET NIGHT

When I contemplate
the sky, festooned with countless lights,
then look down at the dirt,
coffined by night,
buried in dream and forgetful neglect,
love and pain
arouse anxiety in my breast;
my eyes, a fountain,
flow, and at last,
Oloarte, I speak, with sorrowful voice:
— Dwelling of noblesse,
temple of clarity and beauty,
soul, born for grace,
what tragedy
keeps you in this prison, dark and dirty?
What mortal ineptitude
pushes truth so far from the senses
that divine good
is forgotten, lost
to false good, in empty darkness?
Man is lost
in a dream, careless of his fortunes,
while with stealthy pace
the sky revolves,
stealing from life one by one its hours.
Wake up, mortals!
Pay attention to your corruption!
Immortal souls,
fit for the genuine,
can they thrive in darkness and deception?
Ah, lift up your eyes

a aquesta celestial eterna esfera!
Burlaréis los antojos
de aquesa lisonjera
vida, con quanto teme y quanto espera.
 ¿Es más que un breve punto
el baxo y torpe suelo, comparado
con esse gran trasunto,
do vive mejorado
lo que es, lo que será, lo que ha passado?
 Quien mira el gran concierto
de aquestos resplandores eternales,
su movimiento cierto,
sus passos desiguales
y en proporción concorde tan iguales;
 la luna cómo mueve
la plateada rueda, y va en pos della
la luz do el saber llueve,
y la graciosa estrella
de amor la sigue reluciente y bella;
 y cómo otro camino
prosigue el sanguinoso Marte ayrado,
y el Iúpiter benino,
de bienes mil cercado,
serena el cielo con su rayo amado;
 rodéase en la cumbre
Saturno, padre de los siglos de oro;
tras él la muchedumbre
del reluciente choro
su luz va repartiendo y su tesoro:
 ¿quién es el que esto mira
y precia la baxesa de la tierra,
y no gime y suspira,
y rompe lo que encierra

to that eternal celestial sphere!
Scorn the caprice
of the flattery here
in this life with its measures of hope and fear.
    Is it more than one
brief point, this sure, solid ground, against
the great reflection
that gives life its best
present moment, and future, and past?
    Who sees the great concert
of these resplendencies eternal,
its movement confident,
its steps not identical
yet perfectly proportional;
    how it rolls, the moon,
a silver wheel, and light trails after
to where knowledge rains,
and the gracious star
of love follows, luminous and fair;
    how sanguine Mars
angrily pursues another route,
while benign Jupiter
among the good host,
calms the sky with his loving bolt;
    how Saturn strolls around
the summit, the golden age's father;
behind him the crowd,
the luminous choir,
goes, spreading his light and his treasure:
    who can see this
and measure how low this dust lies,
without groans and sighs,
breaking what encloses

el alma, y destos bienes la destierra?
    Aquí vive el contento,
aquí reyna la paz; aquí, assentado
en rico y alto assiento,
está el amor sagrado,
de glorias y deleytes rodeado.
    Inmensa hermosura
aquí se muestra toda, y resplandece
claríssima luz pura,
que jamás anochece;
eterna primavera aquí florece.
    ¡O campos verdaderos!
¡O prados, con verdad frescos y amenos!
¡Riquíssimos mineros!
¡O deleytosos senos!
¡Repuestos valles, de mil bienes llenos!

the soul and exiles us in this place?
    Here one lives content,
here peace reigns; here, established
in its rich, high seat,
a love most sacred
is by glories and delights encircled.
    One sees here
an immense beauty, and here shines
a light clear and pure
that never darkens;
here eternal spring burgeons.
    O countryside!
O meadow, by truth made pleasant and cool!
Richest lode!
O delightful hills!
Restful valleys, of good things full!

5. On the Ascension

"On the Ascension" offers an inversion of "Quiet Night," in which, ironically, the daylight sky is less "illuminating" than the night sky of "Quiet Night." Like "Quiet Night," "On the Ascension" looks up at the sky, but in it the speaker addresses Christ, who has ascended to heaven. In this case the speaker does not see through the stars to the divine, but instead his sight is reflected by intervening clouds back to earth. The same valley that was illuminated in "Quiet Night," in "On the Ascension" is "deep" and "obscure." As with the landscape, so with the soul: the speaker himself, who in "Quiet Night" sees "an immense beauty," in "On the Ascension" is left blind.

Cristóbal Cuevas points out that "curiously, Fray Luis only repeats ... the name 'Pastor' applied to Christ"[1] in one other poem ("Heavenly Dwelling"). Cuevas finds it curious because pastoral imagery is so central to, and ubiquitous in, Luis's poems, and the name "Pastor" enjoys significant attention in Luis's *The Names of Christ*, where Marcelo's explication of the name also illuminates Luis's poetry: Christ, Marcelo asserts, lives in the countryside, and "everything that is in the countryside is the purest in the visible world."[2] His depiction of the countryside is ecstatic: "They are the pure elements, the fields eternally filled with flowers, the sources of the living waters, mountains veritably covered with thousands of very noble goods, somber and withdrawn valleys," and on and

1. Cuevas, *Fray Luis*, 156, my translation.
2. Fray Luis, *The Names of Christ*, 90.

on. "To compare with this region the miserable exile in which we live," Marcelo continues, "is to compare agitation with peace, the disorder, trouble, tumult, and malaise of the most turbulent city with purity, tranquility, and sweetness. Because here one suffers and there one rests; here one imagines, there one sees; here there are the shadows of things which frighten and shock us, there it is truth which soothes and charms us. This is only darkness, tumult, uproar; that is a very pure light at the core of an eternal peace."[3] "On the Ascension" makes that comparison, and laments the "darkness, tumult, uproar" in which we live.

3. Fray Luis, *The Names of Christ*, 91.

EN LA ASCENSIÓN

¿Y dexas, Pastor santo,
tu grey en este valle hondo, escuro,
con soledad y llanto,
y tú, rompido el puro
ayre, te vas al inmortal seguro?
Los antes bienhadados,
y los agora tristes y afligados,
a tu pechos criados,
de ti desposseídos,
¿a dó convertirán ya sus sentidos?
¿Qué mirarán los ojos
que vieron de tu rostro la hermosura,
que no les sea enojos?
Quien oyó tu dulçura,
¿qué no tendrá por sordo y desventura?
Aqueste mar turbado,
¿quién le pondrá ya freno?, ¿quién concierto
al viento fiero, ayrado?;
Estando tú encubierto,
¿qué norte guiará la nave al puerto?
¡Ay nube embidiosa!:
aun deste breve gozo, ¿qué te aquexas?
¿Dó buelas presurosa?
¡Quán rica tú te alexas!
¡Quán pobres y quán ciegos, ay, nos dexas!

ON THE ASCENSION

Will you leave, holy Shepherd,
your flock in this valley, deep, obscure,
in weeping and solitude,
while you, piercing the pure
air, rise to immortality secure?
The ones once blest
but now facing grief and affliction,
once nursed at your breast,
now in dispossession,
in what direction can they turn?
What can they witness
who once saw the beauty of your face
that knows no angers?
After your sweet voice,
what would not be dull and graceless?
This turbulent sea,
who can check it? who can halt
the fierce wind, angry?
If you are cloaked,
what north star will guide the ship to port?
O envious cloud,
will you not suffer us so brief a joy?
Where do you speed?
What wealth you take away!
How blind you leave us, in what poverty!

6. To Our Lady

"To Our Lady" presents itself as a typical example of devotion to Mary, but William J. Nowak gives reason to see the poem as something quite different from that. He points out that, even though Marian piety was quite popular in Fray Luis's time and place, for Fray Luis himself it would mark "a significant break with his otherwise Christological theology," a transition "from a Christ-centered spirituality to a Virgin-centered one."[1] For Fray Luis, this would be "a return to an infantilized type of Christianity that converts the believer into a wailing child searching blindly for maternal comfort in an incomprehensible prison-world," and would offer none of the "intellectual and spiritual enlightenment" of Luis's other poems. The implausibility of so radical a departure from Luis's otherwise consistent theology leads Nowak to propose a reading in which the poem has a countercurrent under its surface. "To Our Lady," then, far from reflecting a sudden devotion to Mary, instead exemplifies Fray Luis's "combativeness under fire, veiled by the ironic appropriation of a popular spirituality that is alien to most of his other works."[2]

Fray Luis accomplishes this irony by maintaining a differentiation between "his incarcerated poetic voice" and "the narration of Marian pieties that introduces each strophe," maintaining them as "two contrasting voices sharing the same poetic space."[3] One

1. Nowak, "Virgin Rhetoric," 499.
2. Nowak, "Virgin Rhetoric," 493.
3. Nowak, "Virgin Rhetoric," 496.

clue to the irony is the speaker's refusal to bridge "the gulf between Virgin epithets and personal lamentation in each strophe," in consequence of which "there is no movement from the realm of the senses, of worldly turmoil and darkness in which the poetic voice finds itself toward the more exalted perspective enjoyed by the Virgin from her celestial pedestal."[4]

The poem's adopting a precedent, Petrarch's 'Vergine bella che di sol vestita,' the final song of the *Rime Sparse*, allows Luis "to sing — to borrow the lexicon of the picaresque — whatever his Inquisitors like," but at the same time to "turn those imposed words into an ironically double-voiced expression of his own. The reader, like the apostrophized Virgin of the last strophe, is asked to read between the lines (so to speak)."[5] Unaided, a contemporary reader likely would miss the irony, but Nowak's expertise helps us "recognize the dual voice that characterizes the poem," enabling us to listen in as "Fray Luis appropriates the discourse of Marian piety in a dialogical way, as just one register in a much more nuanced poetic expression."[6]

4. Nowak, "Virgin Rhetoric," 508.

5. Nowak, "Virgin Rhetoric," 500.

6. Nowak, "Virgin Rhetoric," 505.

A NUESTRA SEÑORA

Virgen que el sol más pura,
gloria de los mortales, luz del cielo,
en quien es la piedad como la alteza:
Los ojos buelve al suelo
y mira un miserable en cárcel dura,
cercado de tinieblas y tristeza;
y si mayor baxeza
no conoce, ni igual, juïzio humano,
que el estado en que estoy por culpa agena,
con poderosa mano,
quiebra, reyna del cielo, la cadena.
Virgen, en cuyo seno
halló la Deïdad digno reposo,
do fue el rigor en dulce amor trocado:
Si blando al riguroso
bolviste, bien podrás bolver sereno
un coraçón de nubes rodeado.
Descubre el deseado
rostro, que admira el cielo, el suelo adora;
las nubes huirán, lucirá el día;
tu luz, alta señora,
vença esta ciega y triste noche mía.
Virgen y madre junto,
de tu hazedor dichosa engendradora,
a cuyos pechos floreció la vida:
Mira cómo empeora
y crece mi dolor más cada punto;
el odio cunde, la amistad se olvida;
si no es de ti valida
la justicia y verdad que tú engendraste,

TO OUR LADY

Virgin pure as the sun,
glory of mortals, light of heaven,
in whom brightest piety glows:
Turn your eyes down
and see a sufferer in hard prison,
surrounded by sadness and shadow;
and if one may know
none more mistreated by human command
than me, here for guilt not my own,
then with your strong hand,
queen of heaven, break the chain.
Virgin, on whose breast
the Deity found dignified repose,
where severity into sweet love was transformed:
If you turned hardness
into ease, you surely can give rest
to a heart enveloped by cloud.
Uncover the desired
face, that heaven admires and earth adores;
the sun will shine, the clouds dissipate;
your light conquers,
high lady, this blindness, my sad night.
Virgin and mother blent,
of your own maker the blessed nurturer,
by whose breasts life is nourished:
Look how much larger
my pain grows moment by moment;
loved faded, hatred flourished;
were they not cherished
by you, where would justice and truth

¿adónde hallará seguro amparo?
Y pues madre eres, baste
para contigo el ver mi desamparo.
    Virgen, del sol vestida,
de luces eternales coronada,
que huellas con divinos pies la luna:
Embidia emponçoñada,
engaño agudo, lengua fementida,
odio cruel, poder sin ley ninguna,
me hazen guerra a una;
pues contra un tal exército maldito,
¿quál pobre y desarmado será parte,
si tu nombre bendito,
María, no se muestra por mi parte?
    Virgen, por quien vencida
llora su perdición la sierpa fiera,
su daño eterno, su burlado intento:
Miran de la ribera
seguras muchas gentes mi caída,
el agua vïolenta, el flaco aliento;
los unos con contento,
los otros con espanto; el más piadoso
con lástima la inútil voz fatiga;
yo, puesto en ti el lloroso
rostro, cortando voy onda enemiga.
    Virgen, del Padre esposa,
dulce madre del Hijo, templo santo
del inmortal Amor, del hombre escudo:
No veo sino espanto;
si miro la morada, es peligrosa;
si la salida, incierta; el favor mudo,
el enemigo crudo,
desnuda la verdad, muy proveída

find adequate security?
Motherhood is enough
to attune you to my insecurity.
    Virgin, clothed in the sun,
wearing a crown of eternal stars,
who walks on the moon with divine feet:
Envy poisonous,
hypocritical tongue, sharp deception,
lawless power, vindictive hate,
all seek my defeat;
but against an army of such ill fame,
what can be this poor, unarmed man's report,
if your blessed name,
Mary, does not take my part?
    Virgin, conquerer
of the serpent that still laments its eternal
pain and perdition, its deceptive measure:
They watch my fall,
the many on the shore,
secure from thin breath and violent water;
some watch with pleasure,
some with horror; the more pious
wear out their voices pleading for me;
I fix my gaze
on you as I face the waves' battery.
    Virgin, wife of the Father,
holy temple of immortal Love, sweet mother
of the Son, of humankind the shield:
I see nothing but horror;
any dwelling I see is full of danger;
any way out uncertain; favor illiberal,
the enemy cruel,
truth naked, but the lie

de armas y valedores la mentira.
La miserable vida,
sólo quando me buelvo a ti, respira.
    Virgen, que al alto ruego
no más humilde *Sí* diste que honesto,
en quien los cielos contemplar desean:
Como terrero puesto
— los braços presos, de los ojos ciego —,
a cien flechas estoy que me rodean,
que en herirme se emplean;
siento el dolor, mas no veo la mano;
ni me es dado el huir ni el escudarme.
Quiera tu soberano
hijo, madre de amor, por tí librarme.
    Virgen, luzero amado,
en mar tempestuoso clara guía,
a cuyo santo rayo calla el viento:
Mil olas a porfía
unden en el abismo un desarmado
leño de vela y remo, que sin tiento
el húmedo elemento
corre; la noche carga, el ayre truena;
ya por el cielo va, ya el suelo toca;
gime la rota antena;
socorre, antes que embista en dura roca.
    Virgen no enficionada
de la común mancilla y mal primero
que al humano linage contamina:
Bien sabes que en ti espero
dende mi tierna edad; y si malvada
fuerça que me venció ha hecho indina
de tu guarda divina
mi vida pecadora, tu clemencia

well provided with defenders and weaponry.
Only when I turn my
face to you does the miserable life breathe.
    Virgin, who to the high demand
gave a *Yes* no less humble than honest,
on whom the heavens like to contemplate:
Like a target
— my arms tightly bound, my eyes blind —
at which a hundred arrows point,
on wounding me intent;
I don't see the hand, but do feel the pain;
neither is given me, flight nor shield.
Mother of love, at your petition,
by your sovereign son I will be freed.
    Virgin, beloved star,
clear guide across the tempestuous sea,
whose soothing light makes the wind barely stir:
Countless waves insistently
toss on the deep a ship, of oar
and sail deprived, on which without care
the damp atmosphere
weighs; the wind roars, the night burdens;
toward heaven it strains, to earth it is locked;
the broken mast groans;
help, before it is dashed onto hard rock.
    Virgin not infected
by the shared blemish of original sin
that contaminates the human line:
It's you I've placed my hope in
since my tender age; and if the wicked
force that conquered me has made me mean,
taken from your protection
my sinful life, your clemency shows

tanto mostrará más su bien crecido,
quanto es más la dolencia,
y yo merezco menos ser valido.
    Virgen, el dolor fiero
añuda ya la lengua, y no consiente
que publique la voz quanto desea;
mas oye tú al doliente
ánimo que contino a ti vozea.

so much the clearer its increase,
and as my ailment grows worse,
I deserve your aid by so much the less.
  Virgin, fierce pain
knots my tongue, which does not consent
to admit for how much I must sue;
but hear my bereavement,
how my spirit calls constantly to you.

7. Heavenly Dwelling

This poem continues Fray Luis's use of music as a metaphor, which Angel Cilveti Lekunberri argues is central to Fray Luis's work. "The concept... that best explicates the poetic *mimesis* expounded by Fray Luis is the concept of harmony interpreted through the concept of christocentrism. Fray Luis give poetic form to this concept," Lekunberri contends, "incorporating the pagan tradition and its heritage on harmony into the Christian notion of grace, which signals universal harmony by the participation of humanity and the universe in Christ: human and cosmos, microcosm and macrocosm exist, relate to one another and mutually reflect the founding harmony of Christ."[1]

Such importance does music have for Fray Luis that Manuel Durán, in discussing the sixth stanza of this poem ("They reach the soul, / the notes of his rebec, their harmonies / worth more than gold, / able to release / one from burdens with their ardencies"), speculates that perhaps "Luis de León's God, at least as described in this poem, is closer to Pythagoras and to the Greek traditions of Orpheus and Alcyon than to the God of the Bible, of Christianity, and of the Christian Platonists."[2] Yet, the speaker's finitude leaves his longing "unappeased." Durán opines that "The final feeling is one of frustration; the poet knows the way, he knows what can be

1. Lekunberri, "Poesía," 159–60, my translation.

2. Durán and Atlee, *Fray Luis*, 71.

found at the end of the long road, but he does not have the strength to travel it, at least not all the way."[3]

This dissonance between the *fact of* harmony and our *participation in* that harmony lends dramatic tension to "Heavenly Dwelling." As is appropriate to "box four," the speaker in the poem recognizes the fact of (transcendent) harmony, but his "longing for divine light and harmony," as Durán explains, "is not fully satisified: the poet is both dazzled by the beauty he is trying to reach and frustrated by the difficulty of trying to reach it."[4]

3. Durán and Atlee, *Fray Luis*, 72.

4. Durán and Atlee, *Fray Luis*, 69.

MORADA DEL CIELO

Alma región luciente,
prado de bienandança, que ni al hielo
ni con el rayo ardiente
fallece; fértil suelo,
producidor eterno de consuelo:
De púrpura y de nieve
florida, la cabeça coronado,
a dulces pastos mueve,
sin honda ni cayado,
el Buen Pastor en ti su hato amado.
Él va, y en pos, dichosas,
le siguen sus ovejas, do las pace
con inmortales rosas,
con flor que siempre nace,
y quanto más se goza más renace.
Ya dentro a la montaña
del alto Bien las guía; ya en la vena
del gozo fiel las vaña
y les da mesa llena,
pastor y pasto él solo, y suerte buena.
Y de su esfera quando
la cumbre toca, altíssimo subido,
el sol, él sesteando,
de su hato ceñido,
con dulce son deleyta el santo oído.
Toca el rabel sonoro,
y el inmortal dulçor al alma passa,
con que envilece el oro,
y ardiendo se traspassa
y lança en aquel bien libre de tassa.

HEAVENLY DWELLING

Ensouled region, shining
meadow, pleasant to stroll in, that hail
does not harm, nor lightning;
fertile soil,
medium of consolation eternal:
Head that stays crowned,
flourishing with purple or under snowfall,
on you the Good Shepherd,
with neither staff nor slingshot,
pastures his beloved flock.
Wherever he goes
his carefree sheep follow; they graze on
the perennial rose,
ever in blossom,
the more consumed the more reborn.
Now up the mountain
he leads them; now at the constant spring
he gives haven,
himself supplying
pastor and pasture of their well-being.
When the sun at the highest
point of its climb makes all warmer,
he offers rest,
and, the flock secure,
with sweetest tones he delights the ear.
They reach the soul,
the notes of his rebec, their harmonies
worth more than gold,
able to release
one from burdens with their ardencies.

¡O son!, ¡o voz!: ¡Siquiera
pequeña parte alguna decendiese
en mi sentido, y fuera
de sí el alma pusiesse,
y toda en ti, o Amor, la convirtiese!

Conocería dónde
sesteas, dulce Esposo; y desatada
desta prisión adonde
padece, a tu manada
viviera junta, sin vagar errada.

O sound! O voice!
If even the smallest part descended
to my dull sense,
my soul, transported,
would be by you, Love, wholly converted!
Knowing your rest,
sweet Husband, no longer a prisoner,
at last released,
it would live in your care,
no longer lost, no longer in error.

8. Respite After the Storm

The structure of "Respite After the Storm" replicates its theme: it speaks of a return to port after wandering, and in its structure it offers such a return. From an opening stanza that includes "seguro puerto," "deseado," and "error," it wanders for eleven stanzas, before returning to port in a closing stanza that also includes "seguro puerto," "deseado," and "error." In between, the threats are manifold: "hidden envy / behind a friendly face," poison, madness. In keeping with the overarching metaphor of a ship at sea longing for port, though, the most pressing danger is that of being broken: three different forms of the verb "romper" (to break) appear in the poem, and they establish a stark contrast between the "uncorrupted light" ("luz no corrompida") the speaker seeks and the ship broken against rocks in a storm swell.

The use of "error" takes advantage of a double entendre that tightens the connection between the vehicle (ship sailing and returning to port) and the tenor (spiritual danger and spiritual safety) of the overarching metaphor. The same double entendre of the Latin root *errare* (to stray) that occasions its giving us the English words "err" (as in "To err is human…") and "errant" (as in an errant knight), gives the Spanish "error" a double entendre that Fray Luis employs here. The ship's wandering is also the soul's sinning: both are fraught with danger, and both are ultimately ruinous unless ended by return to the safety of port.

DESCANSO DESPUÉS DE LA TEMPESTAD

¡O ya seguro puerto
de mi tan luengo error! ¡O deseado,
para reparo cierto
del grave mal passado,
reposo dulce, alegre, reposado!
Techo pajizo, adonde
jamás hizo morada el enemigo
cuidado, ni se asconde
invidia en rostro amigo,
ni voz perjura, ni mortal testigo.
Sierra que vas al cielo
altíssima, y que gozas del sossiego
que no conoce el suelo,
adonde el vulgo ciego
ama el morir, ardiendo en vivo fuego:
recíbeme en tu cumbre,
recíbeme, que huyo, persequido,
la errada muchedumbre,
el trabajar perdido,
la falsa paz, el mal no merecido;
y do está más sereno
el ayre me coloca, mientras curo
los daños del veneno
que beví malseguro,
mientras el mancillado pecho apuro;
mientras que poco a poco
borro de la memoria quanto impreso
dexó allí el vivir loco
por todo su proceso
vario, entre gozo vano y caso avieso.
En ti, casi desnudo

RESPITE AFTER THE STORM

O safe harbor
after my long wandering! O goal,
with sure repair
from heavy past ill,
sweet repose, light and restful!
Thatched roof, away
from enemies, from the need to be cautious
against hidden envy
behind a friendly face,
against perjuring voice, against false witness.
Range that reaches heaven,
so joyous and peaceful that it need bear
no earthly burden,
away from where
the blind and vulgar die in fire:
receive me at your crest,
receive me who flees the madding crowd,
my labors lost,
myself pursued,
my peace troubled, my ills unmerited;
and where it is serene
the air steadies me, while I divest
myself of poison
consumed in my thirst,
but now to be flushed from my corrupted breast;
meanwhile little by little
I erase the memory so strongly impressed
by the lifelong struggle
to leave behind madness,
alternating between vain joy and wickedness.
In you, almost unwound

deste corporal velo, y de la assida
costumbre roto el ñudo,
traspassaré la vida
en gozo, en paz, en luz no corrompida.
    De ti, en el mar sujeto
con lástima los ojos inclinando,
contemplaré el aprieto
del miserable vando
que las saladas ondas va cortando:
    el uno, que surgía
alegre ya en el puerto, salteado
de bravo soplo, guía,
en alta mar lançado,
apenas el navío desarmado;
    el otro en la encubierta
peña rompe la nave, que al momento
el hondo pide abierta;
al otro calma el viento;
otro en las baxas sirtes haze assiento;
    a otros roba el claro
día, y el coraçon, el aguacero,
y ofrecen al avaro
Neptuno su dinero;
otro, nadando, huye el morir fiero,
    esfuerça, opone el pecho;
mas, ¿cómo será parte un afligido
que va, el leño deshecho,
de flaca tabla assido
contra un abismo inmenso embravecido?
    ¡Ay, otra vez, y ciento
otras, seguro puerto deseado!:
No me falte tu assiento,
y falte quanto amado,
quanto del ciego error es cudiciado.

from the corporal veil, almost from the knot
of habit unbound,
I will break out
into joy, peace, uncorrupted light.
    I will contemplate
the predicament of that miserable band
now separate
from you, far from land,
tossed by waves, at the sea's command:
    one ship, long at rest
contentedly in port, now tosses
with each brave gust
in stormy open seas,
against such turbulence defenseless;
    another is broken
on a hidden rock, another victim
the sea has taken;
for another, winds are calm;
another has settled to the bottom;
    others, to clear day
clinging, to forestall the downpour's wrath
try to buy off greedy
Neptune with a tithe;
another tries to swim away from fierce death,
    straining against
the current; but how is the afflicted one
supposed to resist,
once his ship's hull is broken
against the immense, surging ocean?
    Another time, a hundred
other times, I longed for secure port!
Please don't withhold
your loving support
that wards off greed and blind deceit.

9. Another Mode

As with any poetry, it is possible to read too much into Fray Luis's poems. Terence O'Reilly cites as one example Catherine Swietlicki's reading of the first few lines of this poem, which she says depicts Luis's friend Salinas "as a mystic wearing a garment of light,"[1] a depiction she finds significant because such an image recurs frequently in the cabala. O'Reilly disagrees: "surely," he asserts, "it is not Salinas whom the light is said to clothe, but the air around him."[2]

It is *not* overreading, though, to notice that the first stanza employs synaesthesia. The beauty of (aural) music is represented by the beauty of (visual) light. Synaesthesia in the opening stanza then receives its complement, *an*aesthesia, in the final stanza, where the speaker exclaims, "O continue, Salinas, / to sound out for my ears these harmonies / that to divine grace / awaken my senses, / anaesthetizing them to all else!"

Synaesthesia, the joining together of two senses, is only one of the kinds of synthesis Fray Luis practices in his poetry, or even in this particular poem. Colin P. Thompson identifies an instance in this poem of another kind of synthesis: "The sphere music of the classical heavens becomes the divine music of the Christian God; the music of the world below, played in time, with a beginning and an ending, is a distant echo of the music of heaven, out of which it flows in a fragmented and limited measure, retaining only the

1. Swietlicki, *Spanish Christian Cabala*, 173.

2. O'Reilly, Review of Swietlicki, 500.

power to arouse the soul to memory of its source."[3] Thompson correlates this poem's treatment of finite, temporal music as an inadequate but evocative signifier of infinite, eternal music with Luis's use of related imagery in others of his poems. "Images which express what is partial, transient and mortal on earth characteristically but also paradoxically represent what is eternal in the realm of truth," and oblige us to "learn to respond sensitively," recognizing these images as "signposts to the life of heaven."[4] Such a reading suits Luis's Augustinian affiliation, and also concurs with my view that Luis is engaged in "box four thinking."

3. Thompson, *The Strife of Tongues*, 255.

4. Thompson, *The Strife of Tongues*, 255.

A FRANCISCO DE SALINAS

El ayre se serena
y viste de hermosura y luz no usada,
Salinas, quando suena
la música estremada,
por vuestra sabia mano governada.
A cuyo son divino
el alma, que en olvido está sumida,
torna a cobrar el tino
y memoria perdida,
de su origen primera esclarecida.
Y como se conoce,
en suerte y pensamiento se mejora;
el oro desconoce
que el vulgo vil adora,
la velleza caduca engañadora,
Traspassa el ayre todo
hasta llegar a la más alta esfera,
y oye allí otro modo
de no perecedera
música, que es la fuente y la primera.
Y como está compuesta
de números concordes, luego embía
consonante respuesta;
y entrambas a porfía
mezclan una dulcíssima armonía.
Aquí la alma navega
por un mar de dulçura, y finalmente
en él ansí se anega,
que ningún accidente
estraño y peregrino oye y siente.
¡O desmayo dichoso!,

ANOTHER MODE

To Francisco de Salinas

The air grows serene,
robed in beauty and light, pristine,
Salinas, when
rare music sounds,
conducted by your expert hand.
In divine resonance
my soul, normally immersed in oblivion,
recovers sense
and lost recollection
of its source, its illustrious origin.
Thus reminded,
it grows in wisdom and in favor;
it ignores the gold
adored by others
for its deceptive, tarnished luster.
Leaving air below,
it reaches the highest sphere, and hears
another mode,
music that does
not perish, that is the fountain and the source.
Composed as it is
of concordant numbers, the soul conveys
consonant response;
and the two steadfastly
conjoin in the sweetest of harmonies.
Here in an ocean
of sweetness the soul sails, finally
overwhelmed, with no one
to hear or see
an accident so strange and unlikely.
O happy collapse!,

¡o muerte que das vida!, ¡o dulce olvido!:
!Durasse en tu reposo
sin ser restituido
jamás aqueste baxo y vil sentido!
    A este bien os llamo,
gloria del apolíneo sacro choro,
amigos a quien amo
sobre todo tesoro,
que todo lo visible es triste lloro.
    ¡O, suene de contino
Salinas, vuestro son en mis oydos,
por quien al bien divino
despiertan los sentidos,
quedando a lo demás adormecidos!

O death that gives life!, O sweet oblivion!:
Let me persist in your rest,
not be forced to return,
ever, to base and vile sensation.
    To this bliss I call
you, the glory of Apollo's sacred choir,
friends who beyond all
other wealth I adore,
since all we can see is a vale of tears.
    O continue, Salinas,
to sound out for my ears these harmonies
that to divine grace
awaken my senses,
anaesthetizing them to all else!

10. Of Magdalene: To a Woman Past Her Youth

Colin P. Thompson observes the close relationship between Horace's Ode 4.13, in which Horace writes "in a cruel and mocking way of a woman once beautiful."[1] Horace's speaker alerts the woman that "you have become an old / Woman" (as if she would not have been aware of such a thing!). Yet, he goes on, "you claim beauty / Still, cavorting and drinking still, // Still with quavering voice drunkenly coaxing dulled / Cupid's listless approach."[2] He continues by comparing her to another woman, who replaced her in the speaker's affections but died young, leaving the older woman to live into old age, "affording our hot- blooded young men a sight / Fit for gales of their laughter, / How to ashes a torch may burn."[3]

Like Horace, Fray Luis addresses an aging woman, and as Thompson points out he "retains some of the Horatian imagery and themes: the snow of white hairs, the blackened teeth, the suitors who have abandoned her, the passage of time, swift as a bird's flight."[4] But — here is Thompson's point — "the whole Horatian tone is replaced with a Christian morality." The stakes are not sexual love: do the hot-blooded young men pursue me or make

1. Thompson, *The Strife of Tongues*, 237.
2. Horace, *Complete Works*, 333.
3. Horace, *Complete Works*, 334.
4. Thompson, *The Strife of Tongues*, 237.

fun of me? Instead, the stakes are divine love: the permanent and secure in place of the transitory and fickle.

Luis's speaker extends this departure from Horace, by offering Mary Magdalene as his example of a person who chose wisely: "even though lost / and surely damned, / she hastily doused / the *more* ardent fire with the fire that is *most*: // wicked love's hot / flames with the love whose flames are hottest." The moral lesson is inculcated by contrast. Elisa, the woman addressed in the poem, is left with nothing from her past beauty and past loves but misery: "you remain / given over to your burning pain." Magdalene, though, having chosen divine love, receives "the wisdom the perfect / doctor alone prescribes, / the salve that soothes for a thousand centuries."

DE LA MAGDALENA. A UNA SEÑORA PASADA LA MOCEDAD.

Elisa, ya el preciado
cabello, que del oro escarnio hazía,
la nieve ha varïado;
¡ay!, ¿yo no te dezía:
«Recoge, Elisa, el pie, que buela el día»?
Ya los que prometían
durar en tu servicio eternamente,
ingratos se desvían
por no mirar la frente
con rugas, y afeado el negro diente.
¿Qué tienes del passado
tiempo sino dolor? ¿Quál es el fruto
que tu labor te ha dado,
si no es tristeza y luto,
y el alma hecha sierva a vicio bruto?
¿Qué fe te guarda el vano
por quien tú no guardaste la devida
a tu bien soberano;
por quien, mal proveída,
perdiste de tu seno la querida
prenda; por quien velaste;
por quien ardiste en zelos; por quien uno
el cielo fatigaste
con gemido importuno;
por quien nunca tuviste acuerdo alguno
de ti mesma? Y agora,
rico de tus despojos, más ligero
que el ave, huye; y adora
a Lida, el lisonjero;
tú quedas entregada al dolo fiero.

OF MAGDALENE: TO A WOMAN PAST HER YOUTH

Elisa, your hair, though
once of such beauty that for gold it had scorn,
has turned to snow.
Ay, did I not warn,
"Seize your day, Elisa, it's soon gone"?
Now those sworn to stay
forever in your service,
ungrateful, turn away
from your wrinkled face
and your teeth, black and carious.
What except pain
has the past left you? What else
has your labor given
than grief and sadness,
and your soul in service to base vice?
What faith does he hold to,
the vain one from whom you did not withhold
your sovereign virtue;
to whom you, ill prepared,
sacrificed of your womb the revered
integrity; for whom then
you were sleepless, ardent; for whom alone
you worried heaven
with importuning moan;
for whose sake all care of yourself you abandoned?
And now, made wealthier
by your losses, flying freer than
a bird, he praises — the flatterer —
Lida; you remain
given over to your burning pain.

¡O, quánto mejor fuera
el don de hermosura, que del cielo
te vino, a cuyo era
avello dado en velo
santo, guardado bien del polvo y suelo!

Mas hora no ay tardía,
¡tanto nos es el cielo pïadoso!,
mientras que dura el día.
El pecho erboroso,
en breve, del dolor saca reposo.

Que la gentil señora
de Mágdalo, bien que perdidamente
dañada, en breve hora
con el amor ferviente
las llamas apagó del fuego ardiente:

las llamas del malvado
amor con otro amor más encendido;
y consiguió el estado
que no fue concedido
al huésped arrogante, en bien fingido;

de amor guiada y pena,
penetra el techo estraño, y atrevida
ofrécese a la agena
presencia, y sabia olvida
el ojo mofador. Buscó la vida,

y, toda derrocada
a los divinos pies, que la traían,
lo que la en sí fiada
gente olvidado avían,
sus manos, voca y ojos lo hazían;

lavava larga en lloro
al que su torpe mal lavando estava;
limpiava, con el oro

Much better had been
the gift of beauty, that from heaven came
to you, given
in holy form,
protected well from dust and grime!
We need not wait
— so kindly by heaven are we blessed —
to the final sunset.
The seething breast
from its pain gets immediate rest.
That is how kind
Magdalene is, that even though lost
and surely damned,
she hastily doused
the *more* ardent fire with the fire that is *most*:
wicked love's hot
flames with the love whose flames are hottest;
and attained a state
that the arrogant guest
could not attain with his feigned goodness;
guided by pain
and love, she breaches a foreign roof,
and bravely to the alien
presence there offers herself,
in spite of mocking eyes. She sought life,
and threw herself down
at the divine feet that drew her,
and unlike the one
who is his own master,
did what her hands, mouth, and eyes were made for:
she washed with her tears
he who would wash away her sinfulness;
with her golden tresses

que la cabeça ornava,
a su limpieza, y paz a su paz dava.
　　Dezía: — Solo amparo
de la miseria, extrema medicina
de mi salud, reparo
de tanto mal, inclina
aqueste cieno tu piedad divina.
　　¡Ay!, ¿qué podrá ofrecerte
quien todo lo perdió? Aquestas manos
osadas de ofenderte,
aquestos ojos vanos
te ofrezco, y estos labios tan profanos.
　　La que sudó en tu ofensa
trabaje en tu servicio, y de mis males
proceda mi defensa;
mis ojos, dos mortales
fraguas, dos fuentes sean manantiales.
　　Bañen tus pies mis ojos,
límpienlos mis cabellos; de tormento
mi boca, y red de enojos,
les dé besos sin cuento;
y lo que me condena te presento:
　　preséntote un sujeto
tan mortalmente herido, qual conviene,
do un médico perfeto
de quanto saber tiene
dé muestra que por siglos mil resuene.

she cleaned the source
of her cleanness, and it gave peace to her peace.
    She said: — Sole protection
from misery, strongest medicine,
reparation
for evil, incline
to this mud your feet, though they be divine.
    What can one give, who
has lost everything? These hands,
though they offend you,
I offer, these eyes
though vain, and, though profane, these lips.
    What sweated in offense
let it labor now in service; let my sins
issue my defense;
let my eyes, those
furnaces, become two flowing streams.
    Let my tears bathe
your feet, my hair wipe them clean; let angers
and torments in my mouth
become countless kisses;
just what condemns me let me sacrifice:
    I give you a subject
so mortally wounded that it requires
the wisdom the perfect
doctor alone prescribes,
the salve that soothes for a thousand centuries.

11. The Prophecy of the Tajo

Cristóbal Cuevas points out that this poem "is based on the parallelism between the causes of the fall of Troy and the fall of Spain,"[1] referring, by "the fall of Spain," to the fall of large portions of what is now Spain from Christian to Muslim control. In drawing the parallel, Fary Luis is inspired, Cuevas notes, by the opening of Horace's Ode 1.15, which describes "that shepherd of old" — Paris — "abducting the fair Helen across the seas," prompting Nereus to impose an "unwelcome calm" that halted the progress of the sailing ships, and to prophesy "the woeful things // Yet to come of the deed."[2] The prophecy is then recounted: "'Under an evil sign / You now voyage with her who will but be reclaimed / By the armies of Greece, swearing your wedlock's end / And an end to the kingdom long // Ruled by Priam," and so on.

As in Horace's poem, so in this poem corrupt personal morality by a leader has large-scale, tragic historical effects. Also as in Horace's poem, so in this poem it is water in personified form that utters the prophecy; in Horace the prophet is Nereus, the "old man of the sea," and here it is the Tajo, the largest river in Spain. (In English, its name is the Tagus; I have kept Fray Luis's *Tajo* throughout, because I needed it for a rhyme in the first stanza.)

The difference between the two poems is that Luis's has two "overlays" that Horace's does not. Horace's prophecy from Nereus gives a "standard" account of the Trojan War, in which Paris's

1. Cuevas, *Fray Luis*, 113, my translation.

2. Horace, *Complete Works*, 150–51.

abducting of Helen leads to the war and the eventual downfall of Troy. On top of that standard account, Luis's prophecy by the Tajo overlays the Biblical pattern of divine history, familiar for instance from the Book of Judges, in which the Hebrew people are depicted as being prosperous and secure until they (typically in the person of their leader) go morally astray, after which (and as a result of which) they suffer until they repent. Additionally, of course, Luis adds the event from Spanish history/legend of Rodrigo's rape of Florinda (a.k.a. Cava) and its relationship to the struggle between Christians and Moors for control of the Iberian Peninsula.

PROFECÍA DEL TAJO

Folgava el rey Rodrigo
con la hermosa Caba en la ribera
del Tajo, sin testigo.
El río sacó fuera
el pecho y le habló desta manera:

— En mal punto te gozes,
injusto forçador; que ya el sonido
y las amargas vozes,
y ya siento el bramido
de Marte, de furor y ardor ceñido.

¡Ay, essa tu alegría
qué llantos acarrea!, y essa hermosa,
que vio el sol en mal día,
a España, ¡ay, quán llorosa!,
y al cetro de los godos ¡quán costosa!

Llamas, dolores, guerras,
muertes, assolamiento, fieros males
entre tus braços cierras;
trabajos inmortales
a ti y a tus vassallos naturales:

a los que en Constantina
rompen el fértil suelo, a los que baña
el Ebro, a la vezzina
Sansueña, a Lusitaña,
a toda la espaciosa y triste España.

Ya dende Cádiz llama
el injuriado Conde, a la vengança
atento y no a la fama,
la bárbara pujança,
en quien para tu daño no ay tardança.

Oye que al cielo toca

THE PROPHECY OF THE TAJO

King Rodrigo
was having his way with lovely Cava
on the bank of the Tajo,
unseen, but the river
swelled with the prophecy it had to deliver:
— To a bad end,
unjust rapist, is your pleasure leading.
I hear the sound
of embittered voices, the bellowing
of Mars, of fury and rage girding.
How much lamentation
these your pleasures cause! For this beauty
which draws your attention,
what a price does Spain pay!,
to the scepter of the Goths how costly!
Miseries, wars,
flames, deaths, devastation, fierce evils
your arms embrace;
endless travails
for you and for your native vassals:
for Lusitania,
for those who till the soil in Constantine,
for neighboring Sansueña,
for those who bathe in
the Ebro, for all of sad, spacious Spain.
From Cadiz already
the insulted Count threatens, intent on vengeance,
not on mere glory,
with a barbarous force
set on harm, full of impatience.
The trumpet blown

con temeroso son la trompa fiera,
que en África convoca
el moro a la vandera
que el ayre desplegada va ligera.

La lança ya blandea
el árabe cruel, y yere el viento,
llamando a la pelea;
innumerable cuento
de esquadras juntas veo en un momento.

Cubre la gente el suelo,
debaxo de las velas desparece
la mar, la voz al cielo
confusa y varia crece,
el polvo roba el día y le escurece.

¡Ay!, que ya presurosos
suben las largas naves; ¡ay!, que tienden
los braços vigorosos
a los remos, y encienden
las mares espumosas por do hienden.

El Éolo derecho
inche la vela en popa, y larga entrada
por el Hercúleo estrecho,
con la punta azerada,
el gran padre Neptuno da a la armada.

¡Ay, triste! ¿Y aún te tiene
el maldulce regaço? ¿Ni llamado
al mal que sobreviene,
no acorres? ¿Ocupado,
no ves ya el puerto a Hércules sagrado?

Acude, acorre, buela,
traspassa el alta sierra, ocupa el llano,
no perdones la espuela,
no des paz a la mano,

in threat sends its fierce peal to heaven,
and in Africa beckons
Moors to the pennon,
in the sun bright, in the breeze open.
    Brandishing his lance,
the cruel Arab wounds the wind,
shouting defiance;
I see, squadroned,
countless troops arrayed in their encampment.
    Men cover the land,
sails and more sails block out the sea,
clashing voices blend
as they rise to the sky,
and darkening all, dust steals the day.
    Quick and sure,
they board their long ships, and bend
strong arms to the oar;
each ship leaves, as if burned
on the waves, its straight wake, like a wound.
    Aeolus fills
the sails from astern, and through the strait
of Hercules
Neptune's trident
cuts a straight path for the fleet.
    Pathetic man! In thrall
to that sweet lap, do you doze
even when great evil
threatens? In your ease,
who watches the gate of Hercules?
    Fast, man, faster!
Cross the high range, claim the plain,
don't spare the spur,
don't slacken the rein,

menea fulminando el hierro insano.
　　¡Ay, quánto de fatiga,
ay, quánto de sudor está presente
al que viste loriga,
al infante valiente,
a hombres y a cavallos juntamente!
　　Y tú, Betis divino,
de sangre agena y tuya amancillado,
darás al mar vezino
¡quánto yelmo quebrado!,
¡quánto cuerpo de nobles destroçado!
　　El furibundo Marte
cinco luzes las hazes desordena,
igual a cada parte;
la sesta, ¡ay!, te condena,
¡o cara patria!, a bárbara cadena.

shake your sword with menace like one insane.
    Fatigue challenges
anyone outfitted in panoply,
and sweat drenches
all in an infantry,
men and their horses equally.
    Betis divine
mingles their blood with our own,
carries both to the ocean
along with the broken
helmets and bodies of noblement.
    Furious Mars
has made it so that chaos reigns
on *both* sides for five days,
but on the sixth he condemns
you, dear homeland, to the barbarian's chains.

12. Life Apart

My translation of the first stanza ("How tranquil life is / for one who escapes the daily grind, / and instead follows / the narrow road / they've taken, those few wise, once of the world") includes a significant compromise. I have translated Luis's phrase "la escondida / senda" as "the narrow road," to connect it to Biblical language through Jesus' imperative, in the Sermon on the Mount, to "'Enter through the narrow gate; for the gate is wide and the road is easy that leads to destruction, and there are many who take it. For the gate is narrow and the road is hard that leads to life, and there are few who find it."[1] This is a compromise because "escondida" does not mean "narrow"; it means "hidden" or "remote."

Fray Luis *does* want "la escondida / senda" connected to Christ, though he makes the connection through different Biblical passages. Luis's most important theological work, *The Names of Christ*, is structured as a philosophical dialogue in which three devout friends, on a summer retreat at a solitary farmhouse, agree to reflect together on the names used in the Bible to refer to Christ. One name to which the friends devote much discussion is "Way." One character, Sabino, opens the discussion by observing that "Christ is called also 'way' in Holy Scriptures. He himself is called this in St. John 14:6: I am, He says, the way, the truth, and life."[2] "Way" here is not "senda" but "camino"; but Sabino in his next sentence makes the connection by citing a passage that explicitly

1. Matthew 7:13–14, New Revised Standard Version.
2. Fray Luis, *The Names of Christ*, 78.

makes equivalent for this purpose the Spanish synonyms "camino" and "senda." Sabino continues: "To this we also refer what Isaiah says (5:8): 'And a highway shall be there, and a way, and it shall be called the way of holiness.'" "Highway" here translates "senda," and "way" translates "camino."

For Fray Luis, then, Marcelo, another of the friends on retreat in *The Names of Christ*, might as well be talking about this poem in this part of his reply to Sabino: "The Christ is not only steps, highway, path, because of the mentioned qualities which are entirely common to three things, but also because each of them has a property which can be applied to His name. In fact, it is steps that are needed to enter into the temple of heaven, a path which leads unerringly to the height of the mountain where virtue resides, and a dry and solid highway upon which one makes no mistakes and where the foot glides along, never stumbles."[3]

3. Fray Luis, *The Names of Christ*, 83.

VIDA RETIRADA

¡Qué descansada vida
la del que huye el mundanal ruïdo,
y sigue la escondida
senda, por donde han ido
los pocos sabios que en el mundo han sido!
Que no le enturbia el pecho
de los sobervios grandes el estado,
ni del dorado techo
se admira, fabricado
del sabio moro, en jaspes sustentado.
No cura si la fama
canta con voz su nombre pregonera,
ni cura si encarama
la lengua lisonjera
lo que condena la verdad sincera.
¿Qué presta a mi contento
si soy del vano dedo señalado;
si, en busca deste viento,
ando desalentado,
con ansias vivas, con mortal cuidado?
¡O monte, o fuente, o río!
¡O secreto seguro deleytoso!,
roto casi el navío,
a vuestro almo reposo
huyo de aqueste mar tempestuoso.
Un no rompido sueño,
un día puro, alegre, libre quiero;
no quiero ver el zeño
vanamente severo
de a quien la sangre ensalça, o el dinero.
Despiértenme las aves

LIFE APART

How tranquil life is
for one who escapes the daily grind,
and instead follows
the narrow road
they've taken, those few wise, once of the world.
Who keeps his mind clear
of the pride of those sure of their state,
who does not admire
fancy things, gilt
or inlaid in marble by hands dark and deft.
Who doesn't want fame
to sing out his name to celebrity,
nor care to claim
the language of flattery
that condemns all truth and sincerity.
How ease my mind
if I'm pointed in the wrong direction;
if chasing the wind
I walk in dejection,
alive with anxiety, deadened by caution?
O mountain, fountain,
river! O refuge remote and joyful!
Foundering galleon,
for peace of soul
from stormy seas, retreat to this lull.
Dream unbroken,
day pure, happy, free from worry;
relieve me of vain
severity
from one who prizes blood or money.
Let me awaken

con su cantar sabroso no aprendido;
no los cuidados graves
de que es siempre seguido
el que al ageno arbitrio está atenido.
    Vivir quiero conmigo;
gozar quiero del bien que devo al cielo,
a solas, sin testigo,
libre de amor, de zelo,
de odio, de esperanças, de rezelo.
    Del monte en la ladera,
por mi mano plantado tengo un huerto,
que con la primavera,
de bella flor cubierto,
ya muestra en esperança el fruto cierto.
    Y como codiciosa
por ver y acrecentar su hermosura,
desde la cumbre ayrosa
una fontana pura
hasta llegar corriendo se apresura.
    Y luego, sossegada,
el passo entre los árboles torciendo,
el suelo, de passada,
de verdura vistiendo
y con diversas flores va esparciendo.
    El ayre el huerto orea
y ofrece mil olores al sentido;
los árboles menea
con un manso ruïdo,
que del oro y del cetro pone olvido.
    Ténganse su tesoro
los que de un falso leño se confían;
no es mío ver el lloro
de los que desconfían,

to birdsong sweet and innocent;
not to the concerns
that always haunt
one who to others' will is compliant.
    I want to live
by myself, to savor the good I owe heaven,
alone, unobserved,
free of love, of pretension,
of hate, of expectations, of suspicion.
    On the slope of a hill
I have planted by hand a garden,
covered in beautiful
blossoms in season
that secure my hopes, make harvest certain.
    As if intent
on seeing and increasing the garden's beauty,
from the breezy crest
in purity
springwater descends, flowing rapidly.
    And then, calmed down,
winding its way among the trees
and across land
in verdurous dress,
it strews the place with various flowers.
    The garden offers
its thousand refreshing scents to the senses,
and each tree stirs
with soothing noises
that put out of mind gold and scepters.
    Wealth let them keep
who in a shaky raft place their trust;
I won't see them weep
over what they have lost

quando el cierço y el ábrego porfían.
    La combatida antena
cruxe, y en ciega noche el claro día
se torna; al cielo suena
confusa vozería,
y la mar enriquecen a porfía.
    A mí una pobrecilla
mesa, de amable paz bien abastada,
me baste; y la baxilla
de fino oro labrada,
sea de quien la mar no teme ayrada.
    Y mientras miserable-
mente se están los otros abrasando
con sed insacïable
del peligroso mando,
tendido yo a la sombra esté cantando.
    A la sombra tendido,
de yedra y lauro eterno coronado,
puesto el atento oydo
al son dulce, acordado,
del plectro sabiamente meneado.

after the north wind and south wind blast.
    Strained riggings creak,
and clear day turns to blind night;
cries of panic
dissipate,
and the sea is enriched by the obstinate.
    With cordial peace
let my poor table be well stocked;
let others' service
from gold be worked,
who don't fear the sea's being provoked.
    Though every other
make himself miserable by pursuing
incautious power,
insatiably thirsting,
let me lie in the shade, singing.
    Lying in shade,
with ivy and eternal laurel crowned,
I'll turn my head
to the sweet sound
of well-tuned strings expertly strummed.

13. To Santiago

IN HIS EDITION OF the poems, Angel C. Vega rightly notes that "this ode has many points of contact with 'The Prophecy of the Tajo.'"[1] In recognition of that similarity, I have placed them near one another, but I have separated them with "Life Apart" in recognition of the most obvious *difference* between them: Rodrigo's vice leads to defeat, but Santiago's virtue leads to victory. Insofar, then, as history correlates with spiritual life, "The Prophecy of the Tajo" narrates sin, and "To Santiago" narrates salvation.

In this poem, Luis need not adapt classical mythology (though he does drop in Orpheus, the Nereids, and Mars), since the legend on which he draws is already a Christian legend. The legend goes that John (one of the sons of Zebedee; "John" in Spanish is "Iago") went on a missionary journey to the northwesternmost portion of Spain, thus symbolically spreading the Christian gospel "to the ends of the earth," since that part of Spain had been named by the Romans "Finis Terrae" (the end of the earth). When John had returned to Palestine, he was imprisoned and killed. The king forbade his burial, but in the night his body was stolen by disciples, and put in a marble coffin onto a small boat, which was driven by currents to the northwest coast of Spain, where Santiago was buried in a small wood.

One might argue that this poem manipulates its source material as little as any of Fray Luis's poems. Luis gives the legend in more or less its received form, taking it as already concurring with

1. Vega, *Poesias*, 530, my translation.

his own themes and imagery, as in the first stanza, where he places himself as Orpheus in the position of Pelayo, the hermit whose singing in the wood where Santiago was buried evoked a shining that earned the place the Latin name "Campus Stellae" (the field of the star), which became Compostela in Spanish. The synaesthetic correlation between music and light, a recurring theme in Fray Luis's poetry, as for example in "Another Mode," also structures this poem.

A SANTIAGO

Las selvas conmoviera,
las fieras alimañas, como Orpheo,
si ya mi canto fuera
igual a mi deseo,
cantando el nombre santo Zebedeo.
Y fueran sus hazañas
por mi con voz eterna celebradas,
por quien son las Españas
del yugo desatadas
del bárbaro furor, y libertadas,
Y aquella nao dichosa,
del cielo esclarecer merecedora,
que joya tan preciosa
nos truxo, fuera agora
cantada del que en Cithia y Cayro mora.
Osa el cruel tirano
ensangrentar en ti su injusta espada;
no fue consejo humano;
estava a ti ordenada
la primera corona, y consagrada.
La fe que a Christo diste
con presta diligencia has ya cumplido;
de su cáliz beviste,
apenas que, subido,
al cielo retornó, de ti partido.
No sufre larga ausencia,
no sufre, no, el amor que es verdadero:
la muerte y su inclemencia
tiene por muy ligero
medio por ver al dulce compañero.
¡O viva fe constante!

TO SANTIAGO

The untamed creatures
of the forest I would move as Orpheus did,
if my song were
able to do what it should
in singing of Zebedee, that name now sacred.
By my voice his actions
would be forever celebrated,
his deeds by which the Spains,
at last untied
from the barbarian yoke, have been freed,
and that blessed vessel,
of such merit that it could light heaven,
a precious jewel
given us alone,
is now with the dweller in Scythia and Cairo sung.
The cruel tyrant dares
to bloody in you his unjust sword;
it was not human advice;
to you was ordained
the first crown to be consecrated.
The faith Christ promised
with ready diligence you now put into action;
you had your taste
of his cup as soon
as he rose, gone from you, returned to heaven.
True love does not passively
endure too long a separation:
death's inclemency
is short interruption
from seeing the sweet companion.
O living, constant

¡O verdadero pecho, amor crecido!
Un punto de su amante
no vive dividido;
siguele por los pasos que había ido.
    Qual suele el fiel sirviente,
si en medio la jornada le han dexado,
que, haziendo prestamente
lo que le fue mandado,
torna buscando al amo ya alexado,
    ansí, entregado al viento,
del mar Egeo al mar de Atlante buela,
do, puesto el fundamento
de la christiana escuela,
torna buscando a Christo a remo y bela.
    Allí por la maldita
mano el sagrado cuello fue cortado.
¡Camina en paz, bendita
alma, que ya has llegado
al término por ti tan deseado!
    A España, a quien amaste
— que siempre al buen principio el fin responde —,
tu cuerpo le inviaste,
para dar luz adonde
el sol su claridad cubre y esconde.
    Por los tendidos mares
la rica navecilla va cortando;
nereidas a millares,
del agua el pecho alçando,
turbadas, entre sí la van mirando.
    Y dellas huvo alguna
que, con las manos de la nave assida,
la aguija con la una,
y con la otra tendida

faith! O true breast, that love increases!
There is not one point
at which he strays;
the steps his beloved took, he follows.
    As the faithful servant,
if left behind in the middle of a journey,
fulfills the requirement
placed on him, then quickly
rejoins his master far away,
    so, swift as the wind,
back to the Aegean from the Atlantic he will
return, having begun
a Christian school,
but now drawn back to Christ by oar and sail.
    There by the evil
hand his holy neck was severed.
Go in peace, blessed soul,
that now has arrived
at the terminus for which you so longed.
    To your beloved Spain
— because the beginning matches its end —
your body you've given,
to light a land
from which otherwise the sun is hidden.
    Across the sea's expanse
the richly laden boat goes slicing;
Nereids by the thousands,
troubled, rising
to the surface, gather, watching.
    Of them there was one
who took care to keep the ship secure:
gave it protection
with one hand, and with the other

a las demás que lleguen las combida.
    Ya passa del Egeo
y buela por el Ionio; atrás ya dexa
el puerto Lilibeo;
de Córcega se alexa,
y por llegar al nuestro mar se aquexa.
    ¡Esfuerça, viento, esfuerça;
inche la santa vela, embiste en popa;
el curso haz que no tuerça
do Abila casi topa
con Calpe, hasta llegar al fin de Europa!
    Y tú, España, segura
del mal y cautiverio que te espera,
con fe y voluntad pura
acude a la ribera:
recebirás tu guarda verdadera;
    que tiempo será quando,
de innumerables huestes rodeada,
del cetro real y mando
te verás derrocada,
en sangre, en llanto y en dolor bañada.
    De hazia el mediodía
oye que ya la voz amarga suena;
la mar de Berbería
de flotas veo llena;
hierve la costa en gente, en sol la arena.
    Con voluntad conforme
las proas contra ti se dan al viento,
y con clamor deforme
de pavoroso acento
avivan de remar el movimiento,
    Y la infernal Meguera,
la frente de culebras rodeada,
guía la delantera

invited the rest of the Nereids to gather.
    Now it crosses the Aegean
and flies over the Ionian; it leaves behind
the port of Lilibeo;
from Corsica it moves on,
chafing to arrive at our ocean.
    Strain, wind, strain;
inflate the holy sail, charge at the stern,
let it not lose its aim
where Abila nearly joins
Calpe, before reaching Europe's end.
    And you, Spain, to evil
destined, with captivity as your future,
with pure faith and will
come to the river:
receive there your true protector;
    for the time soon will come
when, beseiged by hostile forces, the throne
and scepter, the kingdom,
you will see overthrown,
bathed in blood, in weeping, and in pain.
    From the south I hear
the voice issuing a wailing sound;
the Barbary Sea
with fleets is filled;
the coast boils with people, with sun the sand.
    With confidence armed,
the prows of your foes ride the wind,
and with a clamor deformed
by terrifying accent
make the rhythm of their rowing more insistent.
    Her forehead writhing
with snakes, infernal Megaera angrily
advances, guiding

de la morisca armada,
de llamas, de furor, de muerte armada.
Cielos, so cuyo amparo
España está: ¡merced en tanta afrenta!
Si ya este suelo caro
os fue, nunca consienta
vuestra piedad que mal tan crudo sienta.
Mas, ¡ay!, que la sentencia
en tabla de diamante está esculpida;
del godo la potencia
por el suelo cayda,
España en breve tiempo es destruida.
¿Quál río caudaloso,
que los opuestos muelles ha rompido
con sonido espantoso,
por los campos tendido
tan presto y tan feroz jamás se vido?
Mas cesse el triste llanto;
recobre el español su bravo pecho;
que ya el apóstol santo,
un otro Marte hecho,
del cielo viene a dalle su derecho:
vesle de limpio azero
cercado, y con espada relumbrante;
como rayo ligero,
quanto le va delante
destroça y desvarata en un instante.
De grave espanto herido,
los rayos de su vista no sostiene
el moro descreído;
por valiente se tiene
qualquier que para huir ánimo tiene.
Huye, si puedes tanto;

the Moorish navy,
armed with death, with flames, with fury.
    Heavens, under whose watch
Spain lives, to whom its soil is dear,
protect against such
evil, have mercy, never
relax your surety against suffering so severe.
    But, ay! the sentence
is incised on tablets of diamond;
once the potency
of the Goths has decayed,
in only a short time Spain is destroyed.
    What mightier river,
breaking through the dam, uncontained,
its torrent sounding horror,
drowning the fields, sudden
and ferocious, has ever been seen?
    But end this complaint;
let the Spaniard restore courage to his breast;
for now the holy saint,
made another Mars,
comes from heaven to deliver his redress:
    with his sword shining,
he arrives arrayed in full panoply;
swift as lightning,
anything in his way
he destroys and dismantles instantly.
    The unbelieving Moor
intimidated by the rays of his visage,
suffering grave terror,
counts even the courage
he musters to run away as courage.
    Flee, if you can;

huye. Mas por demás, que no ay huida.
Beve dolor y llanto
por la mesma medida
con que ya España fue de ti medida.
        Como león hambriento,
sigue, teñida en sangre espada y mano,
de más sangre sediento,
al moro que huye en vano;
de muertos queda lleno el monte, el llano.
        ¡O gloria, o gran prez nuestra,
escudo fiel, o celestial guerrero!
Vencido ya se muestra
el africano fiero
por ti, tan orgulloso de primero.
        Por ti del vituperio,
por ti de la afrentosa servidumbre
y triste cautiverio
libres, en clara lumbre
y de la gloria estamos en la cumbre.
        Siempre venció tu espada,
o fuesse de tu mano poderosa,
o fuesse meneada
de aquella generosa
que sigue tu milicia religiosa.
        Las enemigas hazes
no sufren de tu nombre el apellido;
con sólo aquesto hazes
que el español oído
sea, y de un polo a otro tan temido.
        De tu virtud divina
la fama, que resuena en toda parte,
siquiera sea vezina,
siguiera más se aparte,

flee. But for those who cannot, the others:
drink tears and pain
in the same measure
according to which by you Spain was measured.
    Like a hungry lion
he follows, sword and hand blood-stained,
seeking more blood to drink down
from the Moor who flees in vain;
he fills with death both mountain and plain.
    O glory, our grand prize,
celestial warrior, faithful shield!
By you the fierce
African is conquered,
who showed himself at first so proud.
    From sad captivity,
from offensive servitude and deep insult
you've made us free,
and in a bright light
of glory we now stand at the height.
    Your sword always vanquished
the foe, whether lifted up in your
strong hand or brandished
by a brave soldier,
a member of your religious order.
    At the mere
use of your name enemies fall;
what the Spanish ear
knows can instill
fear in all others, pole to pole.
    Of your divine virtue
the fame, resounding everywhere,
draws people to you
from near and far,

a la gente conduce a visitarte.
    El áspero camino
vence con devoción, y al fin te adora
el franco, el peregrino
que Libia descolora,
el que en Poniente, el que en Levante mora.

invites pilgrims to visit you here.
    With devotion they overcome
the rough journey, to adore you at the last,
the Frank, the pilgrim
Libya dusts,
the one from the East, the one from the West.

14. To an Absent Friend

THE ABSENT FRIEND TO whom Fray Luis addresses this poem is Don Pedro Portocarrero. "Almost with Wings" depicted Portocarrero as a model of virtue, and so will this poem, as summarized by its fourth stanza: "In your breast you conjoin / all the virtues a good pilgrim might, / and fill us with the divine / and with what is right: / joys by your presence, / worries and sadness in your absence." In his edition of the poems, Vega comments on that stanza: "Don Pedro Portocarrero was able to boast not only of noble birth, but also a series of excellent qualities of intellectual and moral order, that made him one of the great figures of his century. Fray Luis dedicated to Portocarrero his major works and immortalized his name. The encomiums — today in some instances they seem exaggerated — that dedicate those works are heartfelt and ardent; they prove the deep friendship that united Luis and Portocarrero in life."[1]

This poem, like those dedications, is an encomium, which praises Portocarrero in a way that readers might by now expect from Fray Luis: by taking some of the same features of the world that Luis takes as indicators of the divine — mountain peaks, serene light — and introjecting them into Portocarrero himself, attributing to Portocarrero the same quality of witness that Augustine attributes to the earth, the sea, and the animals in the passage cited above, in the Introduction: not of being divine (that is

1. Vega, *Poesias*, 497, my translation.

impossible; we are in "box four"), but of indicating divinity. "We are not your God. Look above us."

A DON PEDRO PORTOCARRERO

La cana y alta cumbre
de Ilíberi, claríssimo Carrero,
contiene en sí tu lumbre
ya casi un siglo entero,
y mucho en demasía
detiene nuestro gozo y alegría:

los gozos, que el deseo
figura ya en tu buelta y determina,
a do vendrá el Lyeo,
y de la Cavalina
fuente la moradora,
y Apolo con la cítara cantora.

Bien eres generoso
pimpollo de ilustríssimos mayores;
mas esto, aunque glorioso,
son títulos menores;
que tú, por ti venciendo,
a par de las estrellas vas luciendo.

Y juntas en tu pecho
una suma de bienes peregrinos,
por donde con derecho
nos colmas de divinos
gozos con tu presencia,
y de cuidados tristes con tu ausencia.

Porque te ha salteado
en medio de la paz la cruda guerra,
que agora el Marte airado
despierta en la alta sierra,
lançando rabia y sañas
en las infieles bárbaras entrañas.

TO AN ABSENT FRIEND

To Don Pedro Portocarrero

Brightest Carrero,
the high white peak of Ilíberi
has kept to itself your light
for almost a century,
and much too thoroughly
withheld from us joy and felicity:
Your soon coming home
shapes our joys and determines
where Lyco will come,
and the Caballina,
the fountain dweller,
and Apollo, singing and playing his zither.
You join the line
of the illustrious best through your generosity,
but such titles, though fine,
are just minor nobility;
you by your conquering
equal even the stars' shining.
In your breast you conjoin
all the virtues a good pilgrim might,
and fill us with the divine
and with what is right:
joys by your presence,
worries and sadness in your absence.
Because you stayed centered
on peace despite the cruel war,
Mars distributed his anger
across the high sierra,
provoking fury in
the entrails of the infidel barbarian.

Do mete a sangre y fuego
mil pueblos el morisco descreído,
a quien ya perdón ciego
huvimos concedido,
a quien en santo baño
teñimos para nuestro mayor daño;
para que el nombre amigo
— ¡ay, pïedad cruel! — desconociesse
el ánimo enemigo,
y ansí más ofendiesse;
mas tal es la Fortuna,
que no sabe durar en cosa alguna.
Ansí la luz, que agora
serena relucía, con nublados
veréis negra a deshora,
y los vientos alados
amontonando luego
nubes, lluvias, horrores, trueno y fuego.
Mas tú aquí solamente
temes al claro Alfonso, que, inducido
de la virtud ardiente
del pecho no vencido,
por lo más peligroso
se lança discurriendo vitorioso.
Como en la ardiente arena
el líbico león las cabras sigue,
las hazes desordena
y rompe y las persigue
armado relumbrando,
la vida por la gloria aventurando.
Testigo es la fragosa
Poqueira, quando él solo, y traspassado
con flecha ponçoñosa,

The disbelieving Moor
put to blood and fire a thousand villages,
and still we offered
to him blind forgiveness,
for which baptism
we received only more harm;
we saw as friends see
— cruel piety! — so we failed to recognize
the spirit of the enemy,
for which we paid a high price;
but such is Fortune,
that it forgets in some cases one must be stern.
Like that serene light
that glows softly, storm-cloud darkenings
will make day look like night,
and winds like wings
will pile up later
clouds, rain, horrors, thunder, and fire.
But then your one true
fear was for bright Alfonso, who induced
most ardent virtue
from his invincible breast,
into the greatest danger
plunging, but emerging as the victor.
Like a Libyan lion
attacking goats on the burning sands,
he incites confusion,
scatters and then descends
upon the shining army,
adventuring his life for glory.
Proof is in the harrowing
battle of Poqueira, when, though alone and pierced
by a poisoned arrow,

sostuvo denodado,
y convirtió en huida
mil vanderas de gente descreída.
 Mas, sobre todo, quando
los dientes de la muerte agudos fiera
apenas declinando,
alço nueva bandera,
mostró bien claramente
de valor no vencible lo excelente.
 Él, pues, relumbre claro
sobre sus claros padres; mas tú, en tanto,
dechado de bien raro,
abraça el ocio santo;
que mucho son mejores
los frutos de la paz, y muy mayores.

he continued steadfast,
and of the disbelievers
drove to flight a thousand banners.
    But most of all, when
the teeth of death, sharp and violent,
brought him near his end,
he raised a new pennant,
and clearly showed
the invincible excellence of fortitude.
    As he outshines
his bright fathers, so you, like him
of virtue a paragon,
embrace the holy calm;
and how much larger
are the fruits of peace, and how much better.

15. Your Ascent

This poem can be read as a correlate of "Almost with Wings." There, the speaker addresses a mentor, one who has gone before him along the path the speaker himself follows. "On the way to [virtue] now, / with light foot he crosses the great space, / noble Portocarrero, / with wings almost, / daring to go before the rest. // He keeps apart / from the crowd. He walks on gold, yearns / for the hilltop, not / distracted by violence / and anger, not by soft, sweet illusions." Here, the speaker addresses a student, one who is only beginning along the same path (a Licentiate is one who has earned an educational credential whose closest equivalent in the contemporary educational system in the U.S. is a bachelor's degree). The speaker offers what is simultaneously advice and encouragement: "Your cautious step / lengthen to conquer the slope, alone gaining / the mountaintop; / there flows the spring / that is both satisfying and purifying."

The poem, though, is not only a celebration of Juan de Grial's achievement and promise; it is also a lamentation for the speaker's own *lost* promise. At its conclusion, it turns inward, with the speaker adding — perhaps as a cautionary note to its addressee, perhaps as a jab at other unnamed addressees, perhaps as a concession to his own self-pity — adding that "I cannot keep up with you" on your journey. If Portocarrero is to be envied for his journeying as if he had wings, the speaker here (who seems closely identified with Luis himself) is less fortunate, having been "attacked in the middle of my journeyings" by "a tempestuous traitor" who broke his wings.

AL LICENCIADO JUAN DE GRIAL

Recoge ya en el seno
el campo su hermosura; el cielo aoja
con luz triste el ameno
verdor, y hoja a hoja
las cimas de los árboles despoja.

Ya Febo inclina el passo
al resplandor egeo; ya del día
las horas corta escaso;
ya Eolo, al mediodía
soplando, espesas nubes nos embía.

Ya el ave vengadora
del Íbico navega los nublados
y con voz ronca llora;
y, el yugo al cuello atados,
los bueyes van rompiendo los sembrados.

El tiempo nos combida
a los estudios nobles; y la Fama,
Grïal, a la subida
del sacro monte llama,
do no podrá subir la postrer llama.

Alarga el bien guiado
passo, y la cueste vence, y solo gana
la cumbre del collado;
y, do más pura mana
la fuente, satisfaz tu ardiente gana.

No cures si el perdido
error admira el oro, y va sediento
en pos de un bien fingido;
que no ansí buela el viento,
quanto es fugaz y vano aquel contento.

YOUR ASCENT

To the Licentiate Juan de Grial

Now the field recollects
its bright abundance, and the sky
with sadness inflects
the woods, makes them empty
of green, leaf by leaf and tree by tree.
Now to Aegean splendor
Phoebus turns; from the short day he withholds
yet another hour;
now Aeolus sends,
blowing hard even at midday, thick clouds.
Now through the skies
the vengeful crane of Ibycus soars
and with hoarse voice cries;
secure in harness,
the oxen pull the plow through the furrows.
The season convenes us
for edifying studies; our good name,
Grial, beckons us
to try to climb
the sacred mountain toward the final flame.
Your cautious step
lengthen to conquer the slope, alone gaining
the mountaintop;
there flows the spring
that is both satisfying and purifying.
Don't fret the lust
for gold, the thirst for self-deception
in the wanderer, lost;
no breeze sustains
where contentment is fugitive and vain.

Escrive lo que Febo
te dicta favorable, que lo antigo
iguala y passa el nuevo
estilo; y, caro amigo,
no esperes que podré atener contigo.

Que yo, de un torbellino
traidor acometido, y derrocado
del medio del camino
al hondo, el plectro amado
y del buelo las alas he quebrado.

What Phoebus offers,
write, for what is old equals the new
or even surpasses
it, but, dear friend, know
that I cannot keep up with you:
a tempestuous traitor
attacked in the middle of my journeyings
beside the river,
snapping my strings
and, with the same fury, breaking my wings.

16. With a Hundred Voices, With Swift Flight

As WITH SEVERAL OF Fray Luis's other poems, this poem has a precedent in Horace, in this case Ode 3.4. In that poem, Horace tells the story of the revolt of the Giants against Zeus as an allegorical warning of what would come of an attempt at armed revolt against Augustus Caesar. "We know indeed," Horace's speaker admonishes, "How brutal hordes of monstrous Titans / Perished in sudden-descending lightning // From him who gives brute earth and windy sea / Their harmony of order...."[1] His "moral" is that "Brute force and blind revolt, of their own weight, fail: / A tempered force the gods themselves will exalt / To higher ends; they loathe, however, / Force that attempts to accomplish evil."[2]

As usual, Fray Luis turns the source to Christian purpose. Horace finds in the story of the "Gigantomachy" a political/military moral, but Luis finds a spiritual moral, declared in the first stanza: "Not always strong, / Carrero, is evil, nor does poisonous / envy always bring wrong, / and the force that acts from lawlessness / in the end must lose; / in opposing heaven, / the higher one climbs, the farther one falls down." The attempt by the Giants to reach Mt. Olympus by stacking other mountains, Thessaly, Pelion, and Ossa, on top of one another, illustrates the "thesis."

1. Horace, *Complete Works*, 215–16.

2. Horace, *Complete Works*, 216.

For Fray Luis, the relevant battle is not external (as it is for Horace, who warns against a coup) but internal. Evils, he insists, cannot defeat "the constant spirit, / armed with truth," which "on any opponent / steps with its conquering foot."

A DON PEDRO PORTOCARRERO

No siempre es poderosa,
Carrero, la malda, ni siempre atina
la embidia ponçoñosa,
y la fuerça sin ley que más se empina
al fin la frente inclina;
que quien se opone al cielo,
quando más alto sube, viene al suelo.

Testigo es manifiesto
el parto de la Tierra malosado,
que, quando tuvo puesto
un monte encima de otro y levantado,
al hondo derrocado,
sin esperança gime
debaxo su edificio que le oprime.

Si ya la niebla fría
al rayo que amanece odiosa ofende,
y contra el claro día
las alas escuríssimas estiende,
al fin y desparece,
y el sol puro en el cielo resplandece.

No pudo ser vencida,
ni lo será jamás, ni la llaneza,
ni la inocente vida,
ni la fe sin error, ni la pureza,
por más que la fiereza
del tigre ciña un lado,
y el otro el basilisco emponçoñado.

Por más que se conjuren

WITH A HUNDRED VOICES, WITH SWIFT FLIGHT

To Don Pedro Portocarrero

Not always strong,
Carrero, is evil, nor does poisonous
envy always bring wrong,
and the force that acts from lawlessness
in the end must lose;
in opposing heaven,
the higher one climbs, the farther one falls down.
This truth is manifest
in the defeat of the earthy monster
who tried to protest
by stacking one mountain on top of another,
but himself was thrown over,
buried without hope
under the edifice he tried to build up.
If a cold fog should try
to keep from rising the sun it so hates,
and against the bright day
spread its dark wings, it cannot complete
what thus it starts;
it soon burns away,
and the sun shines, bright in the sky.
None to defiance,
now or ever, will succumb: not simplicity,
not innocence,
not unerring faith, not purity,
even if the angry
tiger attacks,
or the poisonous basilisk.
No matter how they conspire,

el odio y el poder y el falso engaño,
y ciegos de ira apuren
lo propio y lo diverso, ageno, estraño,
jamás le harán daño:
antes, qual fino oro,
recobra del crisol nuevo tesoro.
　　El ánimo constante,
armado de verdad, mil azeradas,
mil puntas de diamante
embota y enflaquece y, desplagadas
las fuerças encerradas,
sobre el opuesto vando
con poderoso pie se ensalça hollando.
　　Y con cien vozes suena
la Fama, que a la sierpe, al tigre fiero,
vencidos, los condena
a daño no jamás perecedero;
y con buelo ligero
veniendo la Vitoria
corona al vencedor de gozo y gloria.

in hatred, power, and lying persiflage,
with what blind anger
they purge what is personal, diverse, strange,
they do no real damage:
fine gold recovers
from the crucible its original luster.
    The constant spirit,
armed with truth, dulls the thousand lances
arrayed against it,
dulls even diamond-tipped blades, disperses
all beseiging forces,
on any opponent
steps with its conquering foot.
    And with her hundred
voices Fame condemns the serpent
and the tiger, conquered,
to unhealed, unhealing hurt;
and with swift flight
comes Victory
to crown its triumph with joy and glory.

17. The Sirens

LIKE SEVERAL OTHERS OF Fray Luis's poems, this one adapts Greek mythology to a Christian theme. Here, the stories come from the Odyssey: the bewitching Circe, who changes her victims into swine, and the Sirens, who entice sailors away from their course. In his edition of the poems, Angel C. Vega comments that the argument of this ode "is difficult to determine. It seems to be of what tries an unsatisfying marriage or what attempts to impede the poet, warning a friend of the enchanting deceptions of women and the attraction of riches, from which he ought to flee, if he wants to be saved, like Odysseus. Others believe that the poet warns Cherinto against the flattery of the passions. The last stanza seems to recommend fleeing from women."[1]

The difficulty of determining the poem's argument arises from its conventionality. Vega expects, based on Luis's other poems, a tension with whatever conventional sentiment a given poem relates to; he expects, in other words, that the argument in a poem by Fray Luis will differ in some significant (if subtle) way from a more conventional argument, but here Luis's argument appears to be simply the conventional one. The tension appears actually to be with Luis's other poems, in which the high meadow signals in the direction of heaven. Here, in contrast, a warning replaces the usual invitation: "Watch your step, for the meadow / among its flowers hides the serpent." The meadow becomes Eden, beautiful but inhabited by the deceiving serpent.

1. Vega, *Poesias*, 479, my translation.

LAS SERENAS. A CHERINTO.

No te engañe el dorado
vaso, ni, de la puesta al bevedero
sabrosa miel cebado,
dentro al pecho ligero,
Cherinto, no traspasses el postrero
assensio. Ten dudosa
la mano liberal; que essa azuzena,
essa purpúrea rosa
que el sentido enagena,
tocada, passa al alma y la envenena.
Retira el pie, que asconde
sierpe mortal el prado, aunque florido;
los ojos roba. Adonde
aplace más, metido
el peligroso laço está, y tendido.
Passó tu primavera;
ya la madura edad te pide el fruto
de gloria verdadera;
¡ay!, pon, del cieno bruto,
los passos en lugar firme y enjuto,
antes que la engañosa
Circe, del coraçón apoderada,
con copa ponçoñosa
el alma trasformada,
te junte, nueva fiera, a su manada.
No es dado al que allí assienta,
si ya el cielo dichoso no le mira,
huir la torpe afrenta;
o arde, oso, en ira,
o, hecho javalí, gime y suspira.

THE SIRENS

To Cherinto

That gilded goblet,
Cherinto, with the drop on its lip that still tastes
of sweet honey, fat
for your thin breast,
don't let it deceive you, don't drink to the last,
to the bitter lees.
Distrust the liberal hand; though the bright
lily, the purple rose,
stir the senses when looked at,
when touched, it seeps to the soul and poisons it.
Watch your step, for the meadow
among its flowers hides the serpent.
Just there, where the show
is brightest, it distracts
from the trap so craftily laid out.
You're past your spring;
in your maturity seek the kind of reward
that is more lasting;
from the thick mud
step into ground that is drier, more solid,
before treacherous
Circe charms you, gets into your head,
gives you the poisonous
cup that, instead
of a man, makes you a beast for her herd.
To one who gives in,
unless heaven decides to see you there,
there's no return:
you chuff, a bear,
or angrily snort, a wild boar.

No fies en viveza;
atiende al sabio rey solimitano;
no vale fortaleza:
que al vencedor gazano
conduxo a triste fin femenil mano.
Imita al alto griego,
que, sabio, no aplicó la noble antena
al enemigo ruego
de la blanda Serena,
por do por siglos mil su fama suena.
Dezía, comoviendo
el ayre en dulce son: — La vela inclina
que, del viento huyendo,
por los mares camina,
Ulises, de los griegos luz divina;
allega y da reposo
al inmortal cuidado, y entretanto
conocerás curioso
mil historias que canto:
que todo navegante haze otro tanto.
Todos de su camino
tuercen a nuestra voz y, satisfecho
con el cantar divino
el deseoso pecho,
a sus tierras se van con más provecho.
Que todo lo sabemos
quanto contiene el suelo, y la reñida
guerra te cantaremos
de Troya, y su cayda,
por Grecia y por los dioses destruida.
Ansí, falsa, cantava
ardiendo en crueldad; mas él, prudente,
a la voz atajava

Don't trust cleverness;
recall the wise King Solomon.
A fortress won't suffice:
the mighty Samson
was defeated, stripped of his strength, by a woman.
Imitate the sturdy
Greek who wisely did not abandon
his mast for the entreaty
of the tender Siren,
whose fame in a thousand centuries will not wane.
With sweetest sound
she stirred the air: — Turn your sails,
for chasing the wind
across the seas
is the Greeks' divine light, Ulysses;
come take your ease
here, released from care, enjoying
the thousand stories
of adventure I sing,
as other sailors have been doing.
They all rest here,
soothed by my voice, given satisfaction
for each least desire
by my divine
song, sent home with full provision.
We know the best
tales, and tell the one that all enjoy,
that arduous contest,
the fall of Troy,
by Greece and all its gods destroyed.
Her song was false,
and she, cruel; but he was not lax,
and stayed her voice

el camino en su gente
con la aplicada cera suavemente.
    Si a ti se presentare,
los ojos, sabio, cierra; firme atapa
la oreja, si llamare;
si prendiere la capa,
huye, que sólo aquel que huye escapa.

from his crew with tricks
of his own, the judiciously applied beeswax.
    If she appears
to you, close your eyes; if she calls, stop
your ears. Be wise:
if she grabs your cape,
flee, for only he who flees escapes.

18. Against an Avaricious Judge

As PART OF AN extensive analysis of this poem, David J. Hildner makes two points serve especially well as introductory observations.

The first point is about the "ill-disguised passion" of the poem's speaker. The speaker *does* achieve objectivity in the ethical and theological content of the "message to the powerful wrongdoer,"[1] at least in the sense that many persons would concur with the assertion that avaricious persons actually suffer, or will inevitably suffer, for their avarice. In this regard, the speaker's assertion appears to be more like a schoolteacher's admonition against cheating on a test than like a bullied child's threat that "I'll get you back" as he runs from the bully: a neutral spectator would likely affirm the former but doubt the latter. The speaker does *not*, however, give much information about the crimes that the judge committed.

Hildner's second point is structural. He notes that the first ten lines consist of a series of "five subordinate concessive clauses" (although… although… etc.) that together "build up the expectation of a main clause to resolve the syntactic tension."[2] Then in line 10 "a series of five independent clauses begins; all are negative except the last." This symmetrical, suspense-creating structure culminates in "a summary that not only imitates in miniature the pattern [although… not…], but finally provides an affirmative

1. Hildner, *Poetry and Truth*, 155.
2. Hildner, *Poetry and Truth*, 155.

independent clause that definitively condemns the judge to hell and oblivion."

The combination of these two factors is a poem that by its very structure prophesies the punishment of avarice, not as a contingent fact, a response by one person to the particular actions of another, but as a given, something as inevitable and necessary as the conclusion to a sentence beginning "Although…."

CONTRA UN JUEZ AVARO

Aunque en ricos montones
levantes el cautivo, inútil oro;
y aunque tus possessiones
mejores con ageno daño y lloro;
y aunque, cruel tirano,
oprimas la verdad, y tu avaricia,
vestida en nombre vano,
convierta en compra y venta la justicia;
aunque engañes los ojos
del mundo a quien adoras: no por tanto
no nacerán abrojos
agudos en tu alma; ni el espanto
no velará en tu lecho;
ni escusarás la cuita y agonía,
el último despecho;
ni la esperança buena, en compañia
del gozo, tus umbrales
penetrará jamás; ni la Meguera,
con llamas infernales,
con serpentino açote la alta y fiera
y diestra ano armada,
saldrá de tu aposento sola un hora;
y ni tendrás clavada
la rueda, aunque más puedas, boladora
del Tiempo hambriento y crudo,
que viene, con la muerte conjurado,
a dexarte desnudo
del oro y quanto tienes más amado.
Y quedarás sumido
en males no finibles y en olvido.

AGAINST AN AVARICIOUS JUDGE

Although you stash
in growing piles more gold than you can use;
although this cache
increases because of others' pain and tears;
although your tyranny
suppresses truth, and your avarice,
clothed in vanity,
thrives at market, selling justice;
although you trick
those you pretend to love: you can't insure
against the prick
of burrs infesting your soul; nor the horror
that keeps watch by your bed;
nor will you avoid sentence of agony
as your final reward;
nor will good hope, in company
with joy, your home
ever enter; nor will Megaera,
with her infernal flame,
her serpentine whip that releases terror
from her right hand,
leave you in peace for even an hour;
nor will you end
the circuit, though you apply all your power,
of Time, cruel and hungry,
that comes, with death as conspirator,
to clear your coffers, empty
them of gold and of all you have cared for.
You'll be left to drown
in endless sufferings and in oblivion.

19. Of Avarice

In his magisterial book on Fray Luis's work, *The Strife of Tongues*, on which I have drawn already several times in introducing the poems, this is the first of Luis's poems that Colin P. Thompson cites. Thompson observes that "Fray Luis heaps up images and allusions, under the controlling metaphor of voyages of trade."[1] First, the image of merchants travelling far to bring home spices, then the image of seeking emeralds in mines overseas. "The third verse offers two classical allusions to greed, and from waters as a highway we move to waters as refreshment: Marcus Licinius Crassus, condemned to drink molten gold, and Tantalus, condemned to everlasting thirst in the midst of water."[2] The next verse displays another consequence, miserliness, before the "moral is drawn together in a series of questions in the last verse," questions that are left unanswered.

Thompson then cites a closely analogous passage from *The Names of Christ*, in which Sabino and Juliano talk about misers and wealth and happiness, with Juliano concluding that wealth and happiness are radically different from one another: "Don't you think that gold and silver are something with substance and weight, which you see with your eyes and touch with your hands? But contentment is not like that, it is like something you feel in yourself or imagine you do."[3]

1. Thompson, *The Strife of Tongues*, 15.
2. Thompson, *The Strife of Tongues*, 16.
3. Thompson, *The Strife of Tongues*, 18, Thompson's translation.

Thompson's point is that "the apparently conventional imagery of Fray Luis's poetry is much more integrated with its themes than is often supposed."[4] Its language is such that its meaning is not *only* conventional: it can sustain, and it rewards, being "carefully pondered" and closely observed. And it offers challenge to the reader: "In place of the simple prose technique of questions, answers and exposition, the ode uses a less direct form of communication, with allusions, patterns of images and unanswered final questions, left for the reader to interpret and respond to."[5] In that regard, Thompson rightly sees "Of Avarice" as representative of Fray Luis's poetry.

4. Thompson, *The Strife of Tongues*, 15.

5. Thompson, *The Strife of Tongues*, 18.

DE LA AVARICIA

En vano el mar fatiga
la vela portuguesa: que ni el seno
de Persia, ni la amiga
Maluca da árbol bueno,
que pueda hazer un ánimo sereno.
No da reposo al pecho,
Felipe, ni la India, ni la rara
esmeralda provecho;
que más tuerce la cara
quanto possee más el alma avara.
Al capitán romano
la vida, y no la sed, quitó el bevido
tesoro persïano;
y Tántalo, metido
en medio de las aguas, afligido
de sed está; y más dura
la suerte es del mezquino, que sin tassa
se cansa ansí, y endura
el oro, y la mar passa
osado, y no osa abrir la mano escasa.
¿Qué vale el no tocado
tesoro, si corrompe el dulce sueño,
si estrecha el ñudo dado,
si más enturbia el zeño,
y dexa en la riqueza pobre al dueño?

OF AVARICE

The Portuguese galleon
suffers the sea in vain: no oasis
in Persia, no evergreen
in the Moluccas
can give a troubled spirit peace.
No peace of mind,
Felipe, waits in India, or in
precious emerald;
the soul can't own,
but is possessed by its possession.
The Roman officer
gave up not thirst but life to his taste
for Persian treasure;
and Tantalus
surrounded by water still suffers thirst;
and even worse
is the fate of the miser, taxed only
by the burden of his
own gold, boldly
crossing open sea, fist clenched tightly.
Why accumulate
wealth, if it turns sweet dreams bitter,
if it tightens the knot,
if it furrows the brow,
if on the rich landlord it loads care?

20. Absurd Hopes

Medieval Christian paintings can seem illegible to modern viewers accustomed to representational painting that employs perspective, but they become easier to "read" after one learns that the placement and relative size of the figures is not intended to relate them to the *physical* landscape against which they are depicted, but to the *spiritual* landscape (with divinity or holiness in the center and at the largest scale, for instance). What is being depicted, in other words, is not how things stand on earth, but how they stand in heaven.

David J. Hildner makes an analogous contrast between Fray Luis and "the creators of the modern novel, such as the author of *Lazarillo de Tormes* and Cervantes," for whom (like representational painters in and after the Renaissance) "realism" has to do with how things stand here on earth, and consequently with "the particularity and historical unrepeatability of their characters and situations."[1] In contrast, Fray Luis, though he "often refers to change and mutability," seems "very little interested in describing them, except in the human soul." Consequently, with an effect similar to that of medieval iconography, "he tends to leave behind the fragmentary events that occur once and pass, never to return, for sacred events that combine past, present, and future…."

In this poem, Luis speaks of change (using the verb *mudar*, which like the English word mutability comes from the Latin *mutare*, to change), but (just as Hildner predicts) he first mentions

1. Hildner, *Poetry and Truth*, 9.

change in the external world, but hastily offers a general example or two and then moves to change in the human soul: "Nature changed its law in me." *That* he expounds at more length, employing pastoral imagery (a modest hut in an open field) that by now readers will find familiar.

Thompson notes the consensus that this poem probably was written during Luis's imprisonment, at a point "when hopes of his early release had been dashed," in response to which "he pictures himself as a captive bird whose plight only worsens as he struggles to break free."[2] To which I would add that those circumstances (dashed hopes of release) would account for the urgent repetition — four stanzas in a row — of the speaker's warning to his joys to keep their distance from the prison.

2. Thompson, *The Strife of Tongues*, 77.

ESPERANÇAS BURLADAS

Huid, contentos, de mi triste pecho.
¿Qué engaño os buelve a do nunca pudistes
tener reposo ni hazer provecho?
Tened en la memoria quando fuistes
con público pregón, ¡ay!, desterrados
de toda mi comarca y reynos tristes,
a do ya no veréis sino nublados,
y viento y torvellino y lluvia fiera,
suspiros encendidos, y cuidados.
No pinta el prado aquí la primavera,
ni nuevo sol jamás las nubes dora,
ni canta el ruyseñor lo que antes era.
La noche aquí se vela, aquí se llora
el día miserable sin consuelo,
y vence al mal de ayer el mal de agora.
Guardad vuestro destierro, que ya el suelo
no puede dar contento al alma mía,
si ya mil bueltas diere andando el cielo;
guardad vuestro destierro, si alegría,
si gozo y si descanso andáis sembrando,
que aqueste campo abrojos solos cría;
guardad vuestro destierro, si tornando
de nuevo no queréis ser castigados
con crudo azote y con infame vando;
guardad vuestro destierro, que olvidados
de vuestro ser, en mí seréis dolores:
tal es la fuerça de mis duros hados.
Los bienes más queridos y mayores
se mudan, y en mi daño se conjuran,
y son, por ofenderme, a sí traydores.

ABSURD HOPES

From my sorrowful breast flee, joys.
What trick has led you here, unable
now to have provision or to find repose?
Recall the days when you could travel
with public proclamation, before your realms
shrunk to my small tenure, sad exiles,
where now you will see nothing but storms,
fierce rain and gusts and tornado,
burning gasps and loud alarms.
Here spring does not paint the meadow,
nor new sun gild the cloudy sky,
nor nightingale sing of long ago.
Here night is veiled, here one must cry
over miserable days without consolation,
and today's ill trumps ills from yesterday.
Guard your exile, since this habitation
cannot give happiness to my soul,
no matter how many flights it tries toward heaven;
guard your exile, if when you till
it is joy and rest you intend to plant,
for this field nurtures only thistle;
guard your exile, if you don't want
their punishment, each returning day met
with the cruel whip of that infamous band;
guard your exile, that you not forget
your own being amid the pains I suffer:
such is the force of my hard fate.
Good things, those more desirable and better,
change, and conspire to wound me,
becoming, to oppose me, traitors.

Mancillanse mis manos, si se apuran;
la paz y la amistad me es cruda guerra;
las culpas faltan, mas las penas duran.
Quien mis cadenas más estrecha y cierra
es la memoria mía y la pureza;
quando ella sube, entonces vengo a tierra.
Mudó su ley en mí naturaleza,
y pudo en mi dolor lo que no entiende
ni seso humano ni mayor viveza.
Quanto desenlaçarse más pretende
el pájaro captivo, más se enliga,
y la defensa mia más me ofende.
En mi la culpa agena se castiga
y soy del malhechor, ¡ay!, prisionero,
y quieren que de mi la Fama diga.
¡Dichoso el que jamás ni ley, ni fuero,
ni el alto tribunal, ni las cuidades,
ni conoció del mundo el trato fiero!:
que por las inocentes soledades
recoge el pobre cuerpo en vil cabaña
y el ánimo enriquece con verdades;
quando la luz el ayre y tierras baña,
levanta al puro sol las manos puras,
sin que se las aplomen odio y saña;
sus noches son sabrosas y seguras;
la mesa le bastece alegremente
el campo, que no rompen rejas duras;
lo justo le acompaña, y la luciente
verdad, la sencillez en pechos de oro,
la fee no colorado falsamente;
de ricas esperanças almo coro
y paz con su descuïdo le rodean,
y el gozo, cuyos ojos huye el lloro.

I wash my hands, but they stay dirty;
peace and friendship are but battleground;
sins diminish, but pains multiply;
Ever more tightly am I enchained
by my own innocence and memory;
I fall to the ground when they ascend.
Nature changed its law in me,
made my sorrow something far beyond
my human brain, my best alacrity.
Though the netted bird intend
flight, it tangles itself the more it struggles,
and I am more punished the more I defend.
It is their guilt, not mine, that punishes,
their crimes for which I am imprisoned,
and that seek to make me infamous.
Happy the person never acquainted
with law, with privilege, with the cares
of the world, the high court, market trade,
who, like the pure secluded ones,
to a simple hut withdraws his poor body
and enriches its spirit with truths;
when light bathes all, earth and sky,
he lifts to the pure sun hands that are pure,
that manage without hatred and brutality;
his nights are savory and secure;
he supplies himself agreeably
from a field not surrounded by prison bars;
what is just accompanies him, and the brilliancy
of truth, the modesty of a refined breast,
a faith not colored gaudily;
a lively chorus of rich hopes
and burden-relieving peace encircle
him, and joy whose eyes shun tears.

Allí, contento, tus moradas sean;
allí te lograrás; y a cada uno
de aquellos que de mi saber desean
les di que no me viste en tiempo alguno.

There in happiness may you dwell;
to such a height may you attain;
to those who would know that state well
I give a vision of this other condition.

21. For All Saints

Most of Fray Luis's poems are structured as progressions, taking the reader from one point to another, either conceptually by argument or imagistically by traversing a domain (crossing a sea, climbing a mountain). This poem, though, is structured as an *array*. It is modeled on Horace's Ode 1.12, which begins by invoking one of the Muses, Clio, asking her, "Come, what man or demigod shall you choose to / Hymn with lyre or high-shrilling pipe, Muse Clio, / Or what god?"[1] Horace then proceeds to "hymn" an array of men and demigods. Similarly, Fray Luis uses a question to invoke a Muse, though not one familiar to Horace. "What saint, what glorious / virtue, what deity that heaven admires, / o powerful muse / of the Christian lyre, / will we say, while the sun retires, / taking its bright glow / in hasty retreat, that on this day / heaven shows / among its cavalry?" Luis, like Horace, follows his invocation with an array of encomiums.

By now, though, having seen Fray Luis adapt several poems from Horace, readers will know that the change to a Christian Muse signals a thematic change as well. Cristóbal Cuevas formulates the change well: "Out of the conviction that under the surface of myths there lurk transcendent realities, at which one is able to arrive by allegorical interpretation, and that there is a parallelism between certain pagan gods and heroes and various Christian saints (Diana and the Virgin, Liber and the archangel Michael, Castor and Pollux and Saint Peter and Saint Paul, etc.), Fray Luis

1. Horace, *Complete Works*, 145.

contemplates the Christian saints like a "pantheon" of the divine, in which the heroes of grace assume, sublimated, the virtues of the pagans."[2]

Such a reading finds corroboration in this passage from *The Names of Christ*: "We can therefore say that the stars are a symbol of peace and order, and also a prayer and a hymn of praise to the Glory of God. Each star seems to sing out, each one has her own voice, and all together in a heavenly choir tell us about the wonderful advantages and the shining beauty of peace as it spreads all around us. It is a song without words, a noiseless song. It reaches our souls, it pierces them, it convinces us of the need for peace and harmony."[3]

"For All Saints" is a constellation.

2. Cuevas, *Fray Luis*, 158, my translation.

3. Fray Luis, *The Names of Christ*, 213.

A TODOS LOS SANTOS

¿Qué santo o qué gloriosa
virtud, qué deïdad que el cielo admira,
¡oh musa poderosa
en la christiana lira!,
diremos, entretanto que retira
el sol con presto buelo
el rayo fugitivo, en este día
que haze alarde el cielo
de su cavallería?
¿Qué nombre entre estas breñas a porfía
repetirá sonando
la imagen de la voz, en la manera
el ayre deleytando
que el Efrateo hiziera
del sacro y fresco Hermón por la ladera?
A do, ceñido el oro
crespo con verde yedra, la montaña
conduxo con sonoro
laúd; con fuerça y maña
del oso y del león domó la saña.
Pues, ¿quién diré primero,
que el alto y que el humilde, que la vida,
por el manjar grosero,
restituyó, perdida;
que al cielo levantó nuestra caída?:
igual al Padre Eterno,
igual al que en la tierra nace y mora,
de quien tiembla el infierno,
a quien el sol adora,
en quien todo el ser vive y se mejora.

FOR ALL SAINTS

What saint, what glorious
virtue, what deity that heaven admires,
o powerful muse
of the Christian lyre,
will we say, while the sun retires,
taking its bright glow
in hasty retreat, that on this day
heaven shows
among its cavalry?
What name among these scrublands stubbornly
will replicate
the image of the voice, the very way
Ephrathah could delight
the air when he would play
on Hermon's slope, sacred and breezy?
There, with ivy wound
through his golden locks, he fills the mountain
with the sweet sound
of his lute; taming even
the brutal bear, the ferocious lion.
Well, who will I praise
first but the high and humble, the one
able to raise
us, from the condition
into which we had fallen, to heaven?
To the Eternal Father equal,
equal to dwellers in earthly places,
before whom hell must tremble,
whom the sun praises,
in whom all being lives and increases.

Después el vientre entero,
la madre desta Luz será cantada,
claríssimo luzero
en esta mar turbada,
del linage humanal fiel abogada.
Espíritu divino,
no callaré tu voz, tu pecho opuesto
contra el dragón malino;
ni tú en olvido puesto,
que a defender mi vida estás dispuesto.
Osado en la promesa,
barquero de la barca no sumida,
a ti mi voz profesa;
y a ti, que la lucida
noche te traspassó de muerte a vida.
¿Quién no dirá tu lloro,
tu bien trocado amor, ¡o Magdalena!,
de tu nardo el tesoro,
de cuyo olor la agena
casa, la redondez del mundo es llena?
Del Nilo moradora,
tierna flor del saber y de pureza:
de ti yo canto agora,
que en la desierta alteza,
muerta, luce tu vida y fortaleza.
¿Diré el rayo africano?
¿Diré el stridonés sabio, eloqüente?
¿O del panal romano?
¿O del que justamente
nombraron *Boca de oro* entre la gente?
Coluna ardiente en fuego,
el firme y gran Basilio al cielo toca,
mayor que el miedo y ruego;

Next I celebrate
the immaculate womb, mother of this Light,
the star most bright
in this dark night,
for humans the most faithful advocate.
Spirit divine,
voice unsilenced, breast opposed
to the malign dragon;
not subject to the oblivious,
to defend my life against them you're disposed.
Audacious in your promise,
boatman of the boat not capsized,
of you I profess;
through whom lucid night
passed on the way from death to life.
Who will not regard
your tears, your transformed love, Magdalene,
your spikenard,
the treasure with whose scent
the next house, the round world, is redolent?
Dweller on the Nile,
of knowledge and purity the flower most fresh,
of you now I tell:
in the high desert,
your fortress and your life illuminate death.
Shall I speak of wisdom
and eloquence from Stridon? Of the African lightning-bolt?
Or the Roman honeycomb?
Or the one called
by the people, rightly, *Mouth of Gold*?
Column all afire,
the firm and great Basil touches heaven,
mightier than pleas or fear;

y ante su rica boca
la lengua de Demóstenes se apoca.
  Qual árbol, con los años
la gloria de Francisco sube y crece;
y entre mil ermitaños
el claro Antón parece
luna que en las estrellas resplandece.
  ¡Ay, Padre!, ¿y dó se ha ido
aquel raro valor? ¡Ay!, ¿qué malvado
el oro ha destruido
de tu templo sagrado?
¿Quién zizaño tan mal tu buen sembrado?
  Adonde la azuçena
lucía, y el clavel, do el roxo trigo,
reyna agora la avena,
la grama, el enemigo
cardo, la sinjusticia, el falso amigo.
  Convierte pïadoso
tus ojos y nos mira, y con tu mano
arranca poderoso
lo malo y lo tirano,
y planta aquello antiguo, humilde y llano.
  Da paz a aqueste pecho
que yerve con dolor en noche escura;
que, fuera deste estrecho,
diré con más dulçura
tu nombre, tu grandeza y hermosura.
  No niego, dulce amparo
del alma, que mis males son mayores
que aqueste desamparo;
mas, quanto son peores,
tanto resonarán más tus loores.

before his mouth even
the tongue of Demosthenes must break down.
    Like a tree, the glory
of Francis increases with the years;
and bright Anthony
among hermits appears
like a moon shining among the stars.
    Where has it defected,
Father, such rare merit? What evil
gold has infected
your sacred temple?
In your well-tilled field, who has sown such ill?
    Where the carnation
and lily and the red wheat shone once,
now instead reign
oats, grass, and that false
friend, that pestilent thistle, injustice.
    Infused with piety
your eyes look at us, and with your hand
you root out tyranny
and evil, and plant
instead what is humble, simple, ancient.
    Give peace to this breast
that boils over with pain in the darkness;
that, this ordeal past,
with yet more sweetness
will say your name, your beauty and greatness.
    My sins, I confess,
sweet protector of the soul, surpass
even my neglectfulness;
but as much as they are worse,
by so much will they magnify your praise.

22. Of Moderation and Constancy

The theological works that Fray Luis published after his imprisonment by the Inquisition display an emblem: the image of a tree, closely pruned but with new growth flourishing, with an ax leaning against the trunk, and the image bordered by the text "ab ipso ferro" (which means "from the ax itself"). J. Michael Fulton argues that this is no accident, but a conscious, deliberate selection of "an image and motto that would communicate a clear message to his readers."[1] The source of the motto is Horace's Ode 4.4, lines 57–60: "As tough as holm-oaks hacked with the double ax, / Of boughs dark green on Álgidus' fertile ridge, / That from the very hands of damage / Gather new impulse to life and vigor."[2] This "*ab ipso ferro* motif" — of the harshly pruned tree growing back with new vigor — also occurs in several of Fray Luis's poems, including this one, in which the seventh stanza ("Like knotted oaks / on a high crag, whose limbs are brought down / with a strong ax, / even being broken / by iron only prepares a stronger return") translates Horace's stanza.

What was the "clear message" Luis was sending to his readers? Fulton explains that "the *ab ipso ferro* image was understood in Fray Luis's day to be a jab at his enemies" (18), to the effect of *your attacks have only made me stronger*. Fulton notes the frequency of such jabs at his enemies in Fray Luis's poems: they contain "a total of thirty-six references to enemies and their malice, in nine of the

1. Fulton, "The *Ab Ipso*," 12.

2. Horace, *Complete Works*, 316.

twenty-three original odes."[3] Of this poem in particular, Fulton observes that its "use of the *ab ipso ferro* motif allows us to glimpse the heights of Fray Luis's intellectual defiance." It "demonstrates a very human side of Fray Luis," Fulton notes; "it demonstrates the bellicose refusal to drop his dispute with his enemies and serves as an important contrast to poems in which he expresses discouragement and desperation."[4]

3. Fulton, "The *Ab Ipso*," 18.

4. Fulton, "The *Ab Ipso*," 18.

A FELIPE RUIZ

¿Qué vale quanto vee
do nace y do se pone el sol luciente,
lo que el indio possee,
lo que da el claro Oriente
con todo lo que afana la vil gente?
El uno, mientras cura
dexar rico descanso a su heredero,
vive en pobreza dura
y perdona al dinero,
y contra sí se muestra crudo y fiero.
El otro, que sediento
anhela al señorío, sirve ciego;
y, por subir su assiento,
abájase a vil ruego
y de la libertad va haziendo entrego.
Quien de dos claros ojos
y de un cabello de oro se enamora,
compra con mil enojos
una menguada hora,
un gozo breve que sin fin se llora.
Dichoso el que se mide,
Felipe, y de la vida el gozo bueno
a sí solo lo pide,
y mira como ageno
aquello que no está dentro en su seno.
Si resplandece el día,
si Éolo su reyno turba, ensaña,
el rostro no varía;
y, si la alta montaña
encima le viniere, no le daña.

OF MODERATION AND CONSTANCY

To Felipe Ruiz

What's it worth when one sees
where the lucent sun rises, where it sets,
the hoards of the Indies,
the treasures of the Orient,
the trinkets common people collect?

One person takes care
to leave ease and bountiful wealth
stored for his heir,
but to himself
is cruel and fierce, affording barely breath.

Another, thirsty
for rank and title, serves others blindly;
in pursuit of nobility
forfeits his dignity,
and climbing toward status leaves behind liberty.

One who for golden
tresses and two clear eyes thinks his love deep
buys only frustration,
an hour he can't keep,
but after which he'll ceaselessly weep.

He only is content,
Felipe, who lives in moderation,
to himself sufficient,
who holds no ambition
for anything not already his own.

Neither glorious sunshine
nor cruel Aeolus' invading his realm
will change his expression;
even overwhelmed,
buried by mountains, he suffers no harm.

Bien como la ñudosa
carrasca, en alto risco desmochada
con hacha poderosa,
del ser despedaçada
del hierro torna rica y esforçada.
Querrás hundille y crece
mayor que de primero; y si porfía
la lucha, más florece,
y firme al suelo invía
al que por vencedor ya se tenía.
Essento a todo quanto
presume la Fortuna, sossegado
está y libre de espanto
ante el tirano ayrado,
de yerro, de crueza y fuego armado.
— El fuego — dize — enciende;
aguza el hierro crudo, rompe y llega,
y, si me hallares, prende
y da a tu hambre ciega
su cebo deseado, y la sossiega.
¿Qué estás? ¿No ves el pecho
desnudo, flaco, abierto? ¡O!, ¿no te cabe
en puño tan estrecho
el coraçón que sabe
cerrar cielos y tierra con su llave?
Ahonda más adentro;
desbuelva las entrañas el insano
puñal; penetra al centro.
Mas es trabajo vano:
jamás me alcançará tu corta mano.
Rompiste mi cadena,
ardiendo por prenderme: al gran consuelo
subido he por tu pena.

Like knotted oaks
on a high crag, whose limbs are brought down
with a strong ax,
even being broken
by iron only prepares a stronger return.
Try to bury it,
and it grows back; continue to contend
as long as you want,
but it flourishes, still stands
after he who would bury it lies underground.
Exempted from
any effects of Fortune's presumption,
he is fearless, calm
despite intimidation
by the tyrant armed with fire and iron.
He says: — The fire
that sharpens, even breaks, iron is lit;
for its blind hunger
I am just bait,
finding and seizure of which calms it.
What *are* you, blind to the breast
so bare, gaunt, open? Must you be
a clenched fist,
a heart that knows only
to close heaven from earth with a key?
Push in farther;
try to eviscerate me with your maddened
dagger; aim at the core.
But understand
it cannot harm me, your weak hand.
They broke my chains,
your efforts to bind me: I climb to consolation
on them, the pains

Ya suelto, encumbro el buelo,
traspasso sobre el ayre, huello el cielo.

you gave. In liberation
I soar through the air, ascend to heaven.

23. On Release from Prison

This poem invites comparison with "Another Mode." There, Fray Luis presents the *figurative* release given by music as a metaphor for spiritual liberation. Just as in ordinary language we might speak of music as "ethereal," so in "Another Mode" the speaker depicts himself as transported above air into the ether, in a bliss that anticipates the fullness of divine grace. "On Release from Prison" presents the *literal* release from imprisonment as also a metaphor for spiritual liberation. In both cases, the contrast between a more confined condition and a less confined condition (without music vs. with music, imprisoned vs. retired to the countryside) serves as a vehicle whose tenor is something like divine/spiritual release from earthly/bodily confinement.

The shortest of Fray Luis's poems, "On Release from Prison" might also be viewed as containing in capsule all the rest: grant me release, from confinement by worldly concerns into divine embrace.

A LA SALIDA DE LA CÁRCEL

Aquí la embidia y mentira
me tuvieron encerrado.
Dichoso el humilde estado
del sabio que se retira
de aqueste mundo malvado,
y con pobre mesa y casa
en el campo deleytoso
con sólo Dios se compassa,
y a solas su vida passa,
ni embidiado ni embidioso.

ON RELEASE FROM PRISON

Here envy and lies
kept me imprisoned.
Blessed the condition
of the wise one who retires
from this world's corruption,
who with modest room and board
in the pleasant countryside
with only God around
lives in solitude,
neither envying nor envied.

Appendix: Order of the Poems

HERE I COMPARE ("BACKWARD" and "forward") the order of poems in the current edition with their order in the edition of Cristóbal Cuevas, the most recent Spanish edition of which I am aware. Arabic numerals designate the order in my edition, Roman numerals the order in Cuevas' edition. Because some titles are used more than once, and some poems have variant titles, I use first lines here to identify the poems.

¿Quándo será que pueda	1. X
Virtud, hija cel cielo,	2. II
Inspira nueva canto,	3. IV
Quando contemplo el cielo	4. VIII
¿Y dexas, Pastor santo,	5. XVIII
Virgen que el sol más pura,	6. XXI
Alma regiόn luciente,	7. XIII
¡O ya seguro puerto	8. XIV
El ayre se serena	9. III
Elisa, ya el preciado	10. VI
Folgava el rey Rodrigo	11. VII
!Qué descansada vida	12. I
Las selvas conmoviera	13. XX
La cana y alta cumbre	14. XXII
Recoge ya en el seno	15. XI
No siempre es poderosa,	16. XV
No te engañe el dorado	17. IX

Aunque en ricos montones	18. XVI
En vano el mar fatiga	19. V
Huid, contentos, de…	20. XVII
¿Qué santo o qué gloriosa	21. XIX
¿Qué vale quanto vee	22. XII
Aquí la embidia y mentira	23. XXIII
!Qué descansada vida	12. I
Virtud, hija cel cielo,	2. II
El ayre se serena	9. III
Inspira nueva canto,	3. IV
En vano el mar fatiga	19. V
Elisa, ya el preciado	10. VI
Folgava el rey Rodrigo	11. VII
Quando contemplo el cielo	4. VIII
No te engañe el dorado	17. IX
¿Quándo será que pueda	1. X
Recoge ya en el seno	15. XI
¿Qué vale quanto vee	22. XII
Alma región luciente,	7. XIII
¡O ya seguro puerto	8. XIV
No siempre es poderosa,	16. XV
Aunque en ricos montones	18. XVI
Huid, contentos, de…	20. XVII
¿Y dexas, Pastor santo,	5. XVIII
¿Qué santo o qué gloriosa	21. XIX
Las selvas conmoviera	13. XX
Virgen que el sol más pura,	6. XXI
La cana y alta cumbre	14. XXII
Aquí la embidia y mentira	23. XXIII

Here I compare ("backward" and "forward") the order of poems in the current edition with their order in the English edition of Willis

Barnstone. Arabic numerals designate the order in my edition, Roman numerals the order in Barnstone's edition. In the second listing, the one based on Barnstone's order, I have included his headings dividing the poems into two groups.

¿Quándo será que pueda	1. VII
Virtud, hija cel cielo,	2. XVII
Inspira nueva canto,	3. XVIII
Quando contemplo el cielo	4. V
¿Y dexas, Pastor santo,	5. XI
Virgen que el sol más pura,	6. XVI
Alma región luciente,	7. XII
¡O ya seguro puerto	8. VIII
El ayre se serena	9. II
Elisa, ya el preciado	10. XIX
Folgava el rey Rodrigo	11. XXI
!Qué descansada vida	12. IV
Las selvas conmoviera	13. XXIII
La cana y alta cumbre	14. XV
Recoge ya en el seno	15. III
No siempre es poderosa,	16. XIV
No te engañe el dorado	17. XX
Aunque en ricos montones	18. X
En vano el mar fatiga	19. IX
Huid, contentos, de...	20. VI
¿Qué santo o qué gloriosa	21. XXII
¿Qué vale quanto vee	22. XIII
Aquí la embidia y mentira	23. I

POEMS

Aquí la embidia y mentira	23. I
El ayre se serena	9. II

APPENDIX: OTHER POEMS

Bibliography

EDITIONS OF THE POEMS OF FRAY LUIS

Barnstone, Willis, trans. *The Unknown Light: The Poems of Fray Luis de León.* SUNY Press, 1979.

Blecua, José Manuel, ed. *Fray Luis de León: Poesía completa.* Editorial Gredos, 1990.

Cuevas, Cristóbal, ed. *Fray Luis de León: Poesías completas.* Editorial Castalia, 2000.

Durán, Manuel, and Michael Atlee, eds. *Fray Luis de León: Poesía.* Editorial Cátedra, 1984.

García, Félix, ed. *Poesias completas de Fray Luis de Leon.* Aguilar, 1973.

Tesán, Alda, ed. *Fr. Luis de León: Poesía.* Editorial Ebro, 1942.

Vega, Angel C., ed. *Poesias de Fray Luis de Leon: Edición crítica.* Saeta, 1955.

OTHER WORKS

Aquinas, St. Thomas. *Summa Theologica.* Trans. Fathers of the English Dominican Province. Second, revised edition. Burns, Oates, and Washbourne, 1920.

Arroyo, Ciriaco Morón, and Manuel Revuelta Sañudo, eds. *Fray Luis de León: Aproximaciones a su vida y su obra.* Sociedad Menendez Pelayo, 1989.

Augustine. *Confessions.* Trans. Rex Warner. New American Library, 1963.

Berry, Wendell. *What Are People For?* North Point, 1990.

Brodsky, Joseph. *Less Than One: Selected Essays.* Farrar Straus Giroux, 1986.

Caird, G. B. *The Language and Imagery of the Bible.* Westminster, 1980.

Cancelliere, Enrica. "La celebración de la palabra en el poema de fray Luis de León." In Arroyo and Sañudo. 169–201.

Carter, Jared. *After the Rain.* Cleveland State Univ. Poetry Center, 1993.

Cohen, J. M., ed. and transl. *The Penguin Book of Spanish Verse.* 3rd ed. Penguin, 1988.

Bibliography

Collins, Billy. "Introduction." In Grossman. xv–xxiii.

Florit, Eugenio, ed. and transl. *Spanish Poetry: A Selection*. Dover, 1965.

Fulton, J. Michael. "The *Ab Ipso Ferro* Motif in the Works of Fray Luis de León." *Romance Studies* 21:1 (March 2003): 11–23.

Grossman, Edith, ed. and transl. *The Golden Age: Poems of the Spanish Renaissance*. W. W. Norton, 2006.

Hildner, David J. *Poetry and Truth in the Spanish Works of Fray Luis de León*. Tamesis, 1992.

Hobbes, Thomas. *Leviathan*. Ed. C. B. Macpherson. Penguin, 1968.

Horace. *The Complete Works of Horace*. Trans. Charles E. Passage. Frederick Ungar, 1983.

Kierkegaard, Søren. *Practice in Christianity*. Ed. and trans. Howard V. Hong and Edna H. Hong. Princeton Univ. Press, 1991.

Lekunberri, Angel Cilveti. "Poesía y tradición musical en fray Luis de León." In Arroyo and Sañudo. 135–67.

León, Fray Luis de. *The Names of Christ*. Trans. Manuel Durán and William Kluback. Paulist Press, 1984.

Machiavelli, Niccolò. *The Prince*. Trans. Luigi Ricci, revised E. R. P. Vincent. New American Library, 1952.

Nowak, William J. "Virgin Rhetoric: Fray Luis de León and Marian Piety in *Virgen, que el sol más pura*." *Hispanic Review* (Autumn 2005): 491–509.

O'Reilly, Terence. Review of Colin P. Thompson, *The Strife of Tongues*. *Modern Language Review* 88:2 (1993): 492–94.

O'Reilly, Terence. Review of Catherine Swietlicki, *Spanish Christian Cabala*, and *Fray Luis de León: Poesía* (ed. Fernández-Morera and Bleibero). *Modern Language Review* 84:2 (1989): 499–500.

Robinson, Marilynne. *What Are We Doing Here?: Essays*. Picador, 2019.

Sen, Amartya. *Identity and Violence: The Illusion of Destiny*. W. W. Norton, 2006.

Swietlicki, Catherine. *Spanish Christian Cabala: The Works of Luis de León, Santa Teresa de Jesús, and San Juan de la Cruz*. Univ. of Missouri Press, 1986.

Thompson, Colin P. *The Strife of Tongues: Fray Luis de León and the Golden Age of Spain*. Cambridge Univ. Press, 1988.

Weil, Simone. *Gravity and Grace*. Trans. Arthur Wills. Univ. of Nebraska Press, 1997.